ADVANCE PRAISE

Dr. Marlene Ringler's narrative of raising her son with high functioning autism, spanning his infancy until middle age, is a unique, bracingly honest and fascinating piece of writing. Unlike most other books written by mothers of children on the autism spectrum, Dr. Ringler does not focus on her son's childhood alone and stop there, but instead asks tough, profound questions about what will happen to him as he approaches old age. In addition to describing her own individual journey, she provides the reader with invaluable guidance, for she is a meticulous and experienced researcher with a solid academic background. Dr. Ringler takes an honest and comprehensive look at erroneous and unjust societal attitudes, legislation and institutions in need of reform, as she navigates through the history of autism spectrum disorder (ASD) with a particular emphasis on aging. A gripping and highly enjoyable must-read for anyone who has a child (either young or old), sibling, relative, student, or patient, who has been diagnosed on the spectrum.

Hadas Marcus, M.A.
Instructor of English for Academic Purposes, Tel Aviv University,
Associate Fellow of the Oxford Centre for Animal Ethics

Dr. Marlene Ringler presents an excellent guide for mental health professionals, educators and anyone interested in deepening their understanding of an autism spectrum disorder. In addition, this is a must-read for families facing the challenges of a child with special needs. *I Am Me* includes a comprehensive survey of the latest research and thinking related to autism as well as a revealing personal account of Dr. Ringler and her family. She details the journey of advocacy, support and unconditional love as the family faces an autism spectrum diagnosis. The details about crafting a life for her son, a happy, productive, semi-independent adult are touching to read and a testimony to the commitment of one family to the promise of a better future for a child affected by autism. *I Am Me* is highly recommended for anyone who interacts with adults with an autism spectrum diagnosis.

Dr. Norman Enteen
National Director, Psychological and Counseling Services,
Emeritus, Ministry of Education, Israel

Every mother who has a child on the spectrum has an Ah hah! Moment when it becomes clear that there is a unifying theory which explains why her child is different. For Marlene Ringler that moment occurred when her child was already an adult. Dr Ringler then set out to educate herself about Autistic Spectrum Disorder. She negotiated the change in classification and nomenclature and learned the neurological and psychological underpinning of this unique disorder. She became adept at navigating the various governmental, psychological, medical and educational systems in order to enable her son to achieve his potential. *I Am Me*, a labor of love, describes her odyssey. It is an excellent read.

Harvey Bennett, MD
Visiting Professor, Faculty of Medicine, Bar Ilan University, Safed Israel; Clinical Professor of Neurology and Pediatrics, Icahn School of Medicine at Mount Sinai
Child Neurologist, Goryeb Children's Hospital, Morristown Medical Center

I found this book very moving especially the personal parts describing Dr. Ringler's experience and feelings about her son as he was growing up and also now that he is an adult, accepting him for who he is while at the same time, understanding that he has his specific needs which will require ongoing support from his family and community. I highly recommend *I Am Me* to parents with children and adults with autistic spectrum disorders, particularly intellectually high functioning individuals. *I Am Me* also contains a very readable and clear discussion of the history of autism and the current theories of the etiologies.

Peggy Lewin, MD
Developmental Pediatrician, Jerusalem, Israel

Marlene Ringler's *I Am Me* presents both the inspiring story about a family coming to terms with an autism diagnosis and a well documented and researched professional overview of Asperger Syndrome and high functioning autism. Facing the challenges of dealing with authorities and service care providers, Dr. Ringler tells the often untold real life story of what it feels like to struggle against odds to support her son. For me as a professional dealing with the challenges of adults on the spectrum, one of the most important aspects of her readable book is her call to consider and plan for the future of the aging autistic population once the parents and care givers are no longer around. I recommend *I Am Me* to anyone dealing with an autism diagnosis including family members and professionals. In addition, it would serve as a useful tool for policy and decision makers working to strengthen their support for the adult autistic population.

Arie Syvan, CEO
Asperger and High Functioning Autism Spectrum Disorder
Organization of Israel

I Am Me needed to be written. And it needs to be read by anyone trying to deal creatively with a family member or friend who is on the autism spectrum. I can think of dozens of families in the various churches I served over the last 55 years who would have benefited greatly from this resource. Dr. Ringler tells the story of her family's journey with her autistic son in a compelling yet compassionate and loving way. In so doing she shares insights which will be helpful to anyone on a similar journey.

Dr. Donald E. Inlay
Former consultant to the United Nations in World
Population; former Instructor in Evangelism, Northwest
House of Theological Studies, Salem, Oregon.

With the determination of a scientist and the finesse of an artist, Dr. Ringler simultaneously updates the reader on the state of research in autism expertly interwoven with a biography of her son from a mother's point of view. Marlene has gifted the autism community with a guide that will be useful to parents and others wishing to understand autism from the autism community at large as well providing supports for an individual on the autism spectrum through the lifespan. Marlene shows us that parents are the experts on their children, and, commonality of being human that includes us all.

Stephen Mark Shore, Ed.D.
International educator, author, presenter, and
individual on the autism spectrum

Dr. Ringler combines personal experience—experience of the most intimate kind—with wide-ranging technical and professional knowledge. Readers will be touched by her story, and enriched by her knowledge. This personal narrative is accompanied by news of the latest research on Autism Spectrum emerging adults, embedded in humor, touched with a light-handed melancholy. There is a political dimension to this tale as well: what should our society be doing to bring out the most creative potential in these wonderful people. What is the right thing to do for their families? Marlene Ringler's story includes ideas about actions that are practical and ultimately nourishing to our sometimes aimless educational programs. Professionals in the field will want to read this book, and families touched by these circumstances will find solace and recommendations for action.

Rabbi William Cutter, PhD

Professor of Human Relations; Director Kalsman Institute
on Judaism and Health; Professor of Education and Hebrew
Literature, Hebrew Union College-Jewish Institute of
Religion; Editor and Contributor MIDRASH & MEDICINE:
Healing Body and Soul in the Jewish Interpretive Tradition

I Am Me represents such a huge amount of research and soul searching around the topic of autism spectrum disorders, including Asperger Disorder, as well as Marlene's own roller coaster of learning and experiences as her son has grown up. There are many parents and professionals who can benefit from her experience and her thinking around the many dilemmas parents face in making life decisions for and with their loved ones living with some degree of autism. *I Am Me* will be very welcomed by people searching for help in supporting the adolescents and adults in their lives who are facing similar challenges.

S. Wendy Roberts, MD, FRCPC

Developmental Paediatrician, Professor Emerita,
University of Toronto Clinical Director, Integrated Services
for Autism and Neurodevelopmental Disorders in Toronto.

This is an exceptional book, blending scientific theory and fact with the moving personal experience of a mother who has raised a child—now adult—diagnosed with Asperger Syndrome. It is a "must read" for other parents facing this difficult situation.

Irving Kirsch, PhD

Associate Director, Program in Placebo Studies, Harvard Medical School; Professor Emeritus of Psychology; Author, *The Emperor's New Drugs: Exploding the Antidepressant Myth*

Dr. Marlene Ringler and her son and family's odyssey in dealing with autism is a story of love, compassion, patience, and resourcefulness told through a mother's voice. *I Am Me* is a story of courage and, in no small way, heroism as she intertwines research on the autism spectrum with their decades long personal journey. It is a story of organizations and professionals that hinder or mislead as well as those that do help as her son ages from childhood to his 40's. It is also a story of how to think and create out of the box and never give up. Most of all it underlines two very important and critical actions at the heart of dealing with adversity: love and persistence. *I Am Me* is a must-read book.

Carol F. Edelman, PhD

Emeriti Professor of Sociology and Associate Dean of the College of Behavioral and Social Sciences, California State University

I AM ME

I AM ME

My Personal Journey with My **FORTY** Plus Autistic Son

MARLENE RINGLER, PH.D.

NEW YORK

LONDON • NASHVILLE • MELBOURNE • VANCOUVER

I Am Me

My Personal Journey with My Forty Plus Autistic Son

Published in New York, New York, by Morgan James Publishing. Morgan James is a trademark of Morgan James, LLC. www.MorganJamesPublishing.com

The Morgan James Speakers Group can bring authors to your live event. For more information or to book an event visit The Morgan James Speakers Group at www.TheMorganJamesSpeakersGroup.com.

ISBN 9781683507994 paperback
ISBN 9781683508007 eBook
Library of Congress Control Number: 2017915892

Cover Design by:
Rachel Lopez
www.r2cdesign.com

Interior Design by:
Chris Treccani
www.3dogcreative.net

In an effort to support local communities, raise awareness and funds, Morgan James Publishing donates a percentage of all book sales for the life of each book to Habitat for Humanity Peninsula and Greater Williamsburg.

Get involved today! Visit
www.MorganJamesBuilds.com

Opa, see you in the next generation

~ Your grandson

This book is dedicated to the next generation:

Eden Paz Ringler

Noga Ruth Tagor

Adie Lily Ringler

Yonatan Tagor

TABLE OF CONTENTS

A Word from Siblings

Dr. Mom,

Your telling the challenging story of my brother's development from childhood to adulthood is inspiring. Throughout you functioned with courage, love and determination as only a caring and strong mother like you could.

You relentlessly stared down adversity and defied the odds. You acted with strength, hope and a heart of gold to ensure my brother's wellbeing and development.

Your book is a contribution to families the world over who will be better equipped to deal with an autism diagnosis. They will find inspiration in the story of how you managed to grow my brother into adulthood.

How fortunate for me as well to have you as my mother and mentor. You are my hero.

Yaakov Ringler

For him, I was always 'Pili', his baby sister. We played, we cuddled, we laughed, we cried, we did everything that siblings do and more because he was my buddy. Until one day, he hiked his pants up above the waistline, took his cool looking backward baseball hat off and began singing in the rain on our apartment balcony. That's when I knew. He was different. We were different.

My parents realized intervention was needed to ensure I knew we were different.

By my teenage years, I did.

We each went our different ways and I was able to take a step back enough to understand his disability. I even went on to write academic papers during my university years in order to help me to understand why he says what he says, the way he says it and how it differs from the norm.

I learned that sibling love is unconditional. Eventually I was able to appreciate the challenges that growing up with an older brother on the spectrum presented. And today, my children are lucky to be able to grow up with an uncle who is different. We treasure the life lessons he sets out for us by accepting, tolerating and appreciating people for who they are.

Thanks to my mom, a scholar by default who, by writing this book, is making an invaluable contribution to the field of adults on the autism spectrum. She has taught me the essence of kindness and to never give up learning how to be a better person.

Elana Tagor

Acknowledgements

Many friends, colleagues, family members and the community of persons interested in the subject of adults with autism have played a part in the writing, researching and publishing of this book. Although far too numerous to mention everyone by name, I would like to give special thanks to those whose interest and support sustained me through the many years I spent thinking about my special project. Telling a personal story can be a precarious journey. Thank you to those whose patience never lacked.

Thanks to my editor, Hadas Marcus, for her interest in the subject and willingness to engage me especially during times that I had run out of creative drive and energy. I have benefitted immensely from her encouragement to tell my story. Dr. Irving Kirsch, who is the Associate Director of the Program in Placebo Studies at Harvard Medical School was with me when I began my writing journey. I am the humble recipient of the advice from a respected researcher and writer.

Throughout the process of publishing my book, I have received professional advice from the excellent team at Morgan James Publishing including David Hancock, Founder; Justin Bartlett, Acquisitions Editor; Aubrey Kosa, Managing Editor; Jim Howard, Publisher; Margo Toulouse, Author Relations Manager and Nickcole Watkins, Senior Marketing Relations Manager. I am grateful to them all.

I have been privileged to have benefitted from the insights, kindness, and compassion shown to my family by Offer Dahary, Deputy Director of Shekel, Community Services for People with Special Needs, as well as his committed staff. Thanks and a debt of gratitude to the wonderful companions and guides who have been by my son's side and have been invaluable models for him.

To my children, Yaakov, Ami and Elana. I am forever grateful for your encouragement and unconditional love as I undertook this very personal writing of our very personal story. I honor and appreciate their spouses, Jocelyn and Lior, for always being there and for their warm embrace of their brother by marriage.

Our family benefitted in so many ways from the love and generosity of our son's Uncle Peter. You have always been his most ardent supporter and advocate and have stood by his side during some of his most trying times. I am eternally grateful to you, Peter.

I am grateful to my husband and father of our children, Stanley, for believing in me especially during the difficult times when I lost belief in myself and my ability to mother our wonderful children. You were by my side to debate, critique, and offer insights and suggestions which have proven to be so helpful as I was working my way through my story telling. I thank you for making the time and the space in our lives to push forward against all odds, to defy custom and convention for the sake of our autistic son and to carve out a place in our world which is accepting, inclusive and gentle in order to embrace our child. Your dedication and commitment to the concept of Tikun Olam, working to make the world a better place, was the standard you set for our family and the beacon of hope and faith which guided us through some difficult times.

Introduction

Asperger syndrome is a condition on the autism spectrum that has a profound effect on the lives of the persons who are diagnosed as well as their families. My own introduction to Asperger began over 40 years ago, but its telling begins only now.

Similar to many musings that are waiting to be shared and written, my personal journey roamed in my mind for as many years as I can recall: the story of my Asperger son and my family.

Current statistics indicate that in the United States about one in every 68 children is diagnosed with autism, and one of "those 68" is my son. Yesterday's autistic child, however, is today's autistic adult. And so, as the mother of a 40-plus grown man on the autistic spectrum, I worry about just what will happen to my "child" when I am no longer around to manage, support, and guide him. Who will look after him? Who will care? Who will love my son?

My story began over 40 years ago, but its telling began only yesterday.

Waiting in a line, walking outside with my dog, gardening, shopping, cooking, driving, traveling, socializing, resting - thoughts about my son were often uppermost and indeed drove and informed so much of my life that it has become hard to separate between decisions that were made based upon his best interests or mine, or those of my nuclear family, including my other two children and their spouses, my husband and my grandchildren.

I waited and waited for the right moment to occur, when I would begin the process of telling, until I realized, after so many years, that there would never be a "right moment."

And so, it was on a rather ordinary and mundane morning that I made the decision to begin to share with you, my readers, much about the life of my son, a handsome and intelligent young man diagnosed over twenty years ago with Asperger syndrome also referred to as high functioning autism (HFA) on the autism spectrum.

I worried that no one would really be interested in a story which seemed so banal, the story of a middle-class family living a relatively stable and good life in the Middle East; of children born into a family cherishing the values common to this class, including emphasis on education, respect for others, economic independence, self- determination, pride in one's accomplishments, and the list goes on. The lives of my children were often determined and guided by our own value system. One day, however, much of what we, as parents, may once have assumed to be true no longer is.

A child is born who is different and loveable, stubborn and funny, strange and insightful, articulate and speechless, demanding and thoughtful, generous and frugal, capable and impaired. We are faced with so many contradictions that fit no one pattern described by our pediatrician or detailed in the literature on infancy and early childhood.

Our son was "the sandwich" of our three children. I had a normal, full-term pregnancy and the delivery was uneventful. However, upon taking his first breath, the baby began to howl so loudly that even the professional staff was taken aback by his cries. The early days were filled with frustrating efforts at breastfeeding. Here was an infant who loved to be cradled but refused to suckle.

My pediatrician, a young new immigrant from Cuba, examined him carefully on my first visit to his office with my newborn son. I remembered the first doctor's appointment with my eldest son and wondered why this visit with my second son was taking so long.

After what seemed like an eternity, the doctor told me that there were some issues that might be of concern. He gave me a few details and I was too exhausted and sleep-deprived to ask for more information. We were scheduled for a return visit the following week. Our visits became frequent, his examinations were thorough, and he was kind and attentive. Only after several months did the pediatrician share with me that my son's development would need to be carefully monitored and that I could expect some unidentified challenges as he grew and matured. Again, he was circumspect and ambiguous, but also supportive and gentle, always answering my questions thoughtfully. I began to rely on his professional judgment in helping me to make sense of some of the unusual behavioral and developmental patterns that emerged.

Far too many years have passed for me to be able to give a full, detailed, and accurate description of my son's infancy and childhood, but I do remember several prominent aspects of his early growth and development.

He began to use vocabulary that, at the time, seemed to be well beyond his years, and he did not use typical baby words but actually spoke in almost complete, well-formed sentences. His speech was quite early on in his development, as I recall, but well within the normal chronological age. It was as though his young brain was racing ahead of his development. His intonation, grammar and vocabulary were both startling and amazing to us and we were so proud of what seemed to us to be our child prodigy. We later understood, sadly, that the "little professor" description of Asperger syndrome fit our little boy so accurately.

He was a very handsome young boy, always smiling and cute. While he did not seek out attention, he was often the center of it but, paradoxically, he ran away from social events and people as though trying to be inconspicuous. He much preferred looking at his books, playing with his dinosaur toys, and building with his trucks and Lego.

When he entered a local preschool program he was often the star of the class, as he was easily approachable by his peers though he rarely initiated the contact. He enjoyed expressing himself verbally in a way that was praised by his early childhood teachers. He was, however, often clumsy and unable to play ball. Throwing and catching were hard for him so he preferred to sit by himself and leaf through a book while other boys his age romped on the playground. His clumsiness and preference for things rather than people were early signs of an autism spectrum disorder.

Our son's early years were happy ones. His days were filled with fun activities but while everything seemed quite typical and normal, there was this lingering sense that things were not quite right. He had meltdowns, temper tantrums and a lack of coordination and control that seemed to typify children of his age. However, while these appeared at a level of frequency that the pediatrician described as well within the norm, their intensity and duration appeared to us, his parents, to indicate some lack of a regulating mechanism. During his kindergarten year, the teacher described his learning as atypical and recommended that he attend a well- known pre-school learning center called Kingsbury House in Washington, D.C. By the time he entered kindergarten we had moved from Florida to Maryland and his younger sister had been born.

After he had spent a summer at Kingsbury House, we were called in for a session with the staff. They were straightforward. Our son, they said, had been diagnosed with dyslexia, which precluded his future ability to read at an age appropriate level, if at all. His impairment was severe and they had serious questions about whether he would be capable of learning to read. We were stunned. My husband angrily walked out of the session. I was left with a sense of helplessness and fear. Our son loved books. He enjoyed flipping through the pages and seemed to be fascinated by the letters. The diagnosis appeared to contradict our intuition as parents. It just seemed so ironic and strange. How could a book-loving child be dyslexic? Once again, what we had assumed to be reasonable and true turned out to be quite the opposite. His early fascination with books and letters was perhaps indicative of his curiosity about things that he struggled to understand. We would come to terms with a particular reality. Much of what we had taken for granted about our son was simply untrue or inaccurate. While he did love books, his approach to making sense of a text was non-traditional. His emerging world, pattern of learning and behavior, engagement with adults and family, were different, unpredictable and frustrating to us.

After many years of intensive support and non-traditional methods to help him become literate, he eventually turned out to be a prolific reader. Indeed reading became a good source of leisure and relaxation for him. In addition to building up his vocabulary and teaching him so much about diverse subjects, his great passion for reading led to his years of delving into religious texts. In his later adult years he studied at a Yeshiva, a Jewish learning center, and learned more about his religion and himself as a young Jewish single man living in the 21st century. To this day, he can quote texts and engage in a philosophical debate with great enthusiasm and knowledge. These verbal encounters often become "lectures" as he tends to pay scant attention to the give-and-take of normal conversational rules and conventions.

In 1986, when our son was entering adolescence at age 12, the family moved to Israel. We prepared him for this move as best as we could by setting up support systems to ease him through the difficulty of assimilating into another culture, including mastering a foreign language. He did surprisingly well, at least initially. He appeared to enjoy the challenges of learning a new language. If he acted somewhat strange and angry at times, well, we merely thought that this was his way of dealing with a new environment, cultural differences and having to navigate his way through unfamiliar situations.

Unfortunately, we did not realize at the time and lacked the necessary knowledge about his condition to appreciate how profoundly change affects behavior. We enrolled him in the neighborhood school. Since he was a new immigrant, expectations were low. He was not required to read or speak at the level of his classmates and he was accepted as a good member of his class community. This all changed, however, when he entered junior high school, where academic achievement was expected of him. He did not meet the unreasonable standard of this particular school which did not take into consideration his relatively new status in the country. At the end of his first year, the principal, a retired Israel Defense Forces officer but not an educator, called us in for a conference and informed us that while our son was a "good boy who caused no trouble" he had to leave as he was not able to maintain the standard the school had set for itself. At first we rejected this as being unfair and unreasonable and even protested to the powers that be regarding our son's dismissal. We took it upon ourselves as parents to invite the appropriate authorities to review and reverse such a callous verdict and, later, formed a watch-dog committee of parents to ensure that this particular principal, lacking any formal pedagogical training, did not make any similar decisions in the future.

Again, we were our son's spokesperson and advocate, demanding to be heard and understood. As one parent expressed the feeling, we became "warrior parents". This was a role that we continued to play even as our son entered adulthood. Parental advocacy, challenging the existing order and reliance upon the support, good will and good sense of reasonable people have been guiding principles for us as parents. It was not easy, nor was it always accepted, and surely not a role we would have desired. Children grow into independence we were told in our early years of parenting. Our role as parents is to seek out ways to encourage and support such independence. Tough love needs to be applied. Our son has to reach the bottom in order to work his way to the top. So much advice from so many well-meaning professionals, friends, and family members. And oh, so ill- advised and incorrect and uninformed.

Given this context, I will present a brief overview of the history of the Asperger syndrome diagnosis, in an effort to explain how so many years passed before we as parents began to grasp what we had never understood before: how this diagnosis fit our son. I will then move into the early years of his development, including the environmental and familial issues that directly affected him. Moving chronologically through his development, I will then look at the turbulent adolescent years and how the Asperger syndrome diagnosis, once revealed and understood, informed our decisions about his schooling, living conditions and related family issues.

From adolescence, I will go on to discuss his early adult years and the efforts invested in helping him to reconnect to his native country, America. From there, I will look at his return to Israel and the efforts at stabilizing him through suitable work, independent living, and organizational support. At the point that he has now turned 40, coinciding with the writing of this book, I will attempt to describe his current life, with an eye towards looking ahead to the unknown future.

As his mother, most of what I am attempting to write about my son is personal and private, but I believe that in sharing with my readers my own anxieties and worries, hopes and wishes, highs and lows, I can make a contribution to this ever-growing subject of high functioning autism, or Asperger syndrome. Thus, I will be presenting a point of view that is obviously subjective, while also drawing upon past and current research and development as they inform our parental decisions, our lives, and the life of our son.

It is my aspiration in writing this book to help other parents of adult children diagnosed with Asperger syndrome or high functioning autism (HFA) come to terms with the reality that the world does not always look graciously upon people who are different. I hope and wish that I can support them in accepting this reality and drawing strength, for the sake of their children, to forge new paths of understanding. If I can offer a source of strength and optimism, then this book will have served its purpose.

CHAPTER 1

A Brief History of an Asperger Syndrome Diagnosis

Pioneers of a Puzzling Disorder

It is fascinating to contemplate the history of the development of the current diagnosis of Asperger syndrome by looking at its discoverers and the unusual coincidences that they shared. Hans Asperger and Leo Kanner were both born and raised in Austria, but Kanner moved to the United States in 1924, at age 28. In 1930, shortly after his arrival to Johns Hopkins School of Medicine in Baltimore, Maryland, he was selected to develop the first child psychiatry service in a pediatric hospital in the United States. He became famous in 1943, when he introduced the label "early infantile autism" for a disorder and clinical entity that had been previously unrecognized. It is interesting to note, that case studies did provide evidence of such a diagnosis which had not been named, however, until Kanner came along.

In 1944, an Austrian pediatrician named Hans Asperger first described the syndrome with apparently scant awareness of the classical description of autism, presented one year earlier by Kanner. One of Dr. Asperger's first papers,

"Autistic Psychopathy in Childhood" appeared in a journal of psychiatry and neurology, only to be reprinted for wider distribution nearly ten years later. His papers were written in German, published during the war, and not widely read. Not until Dr. Lorna Wing, a researcher at the Institute of Psychiatry in London, paid attention to his original publications was the term "Asperger syndrome" coined. At that time, the condition we now know as Asperger syndrome or high functioning autism (HFA) was virtually unknown in the United States and non-German speaking countries. Dr. Wing's publication in 1981, which sparked an interest in Asperger's published articles, noted the similarities between the syndrome and autism.

Asperger, who was ten years younger than Kanner, studied general medicine specializing in pediatrics, and was mainly involved with difficult children at the University Pediatric Clinic in Vienna. In his second doctoral thesis published in 1944, he focused on what he described as "autistic psychopathy" or what is today known as autism, a label coined by Eugen Bleuler to describe a schizophrenic patient's loss of contact with the outside world.

It is assumed that Kanner and Asperger, both studying special children, chose this label independently of one another. The term seemed appropriate for the typical disinterest and detachment from the social world they had witnessed in their patients. Kanner and Asperger shared a professional life goal of convincing their colleagues that such a strange disorder did exist, albeit still not identified. They both knew it had been described in case studies, and that this condition was present from early childhood.

It wasn't until 1991, however, that Uta Frith published an authoritative translation of Asperger's work. Dr. Wing had formulated the question which remains at the heart of discussions today, even after the publication of the fifth edition of the Diagnostic and Statistical Manual (DSM-V), and following years of heated debate: Are Asperger syndrome (AS) and autism the same disorder on a spectrum, or are they two separate and distinct conditions? This crucial question has informed and shaped current trends in diagnosis and rehabilitation methods. I must add that, as a parent, viewing AS at the high end of the autism spectrum disorder (ASD), often referred to as high functioning autism or HFA, has given me a helpful framework and a working diagnosis to guide my decisions about my son's welfare and treatment.

To include Asperger syndrome under the umbrella of the autism spectrum can be viewed in light of our current understanding of the research of both medical pioneers in the field of autism. Hans Asperger's refinement of the definition of autism was the outcome of his intense interest and motivation to work with special children, and his contributions arguably influenced the contemporary debate about just where to place Asperger syndrome in the current DSM. Asperger, however, did not use his own name for the disorder he witnessed but rather chose the term "autistic psychopathy", an expression not widely used today nor even recognized as a good description of the syndrome.

Asperger believed that his children suffered from what he saw as a neurological, genetically-based personality disorder which made them an intriguing, but frustrating and difficult, population to work with as they did not fit any known behavioral patterns. He appreciated and was captivated by their special skills, personalities and interests while, somewhat remarkably, he also recognized their simultaneous learning disabilities, social ineptness, and troubling behaviors.

At the clinic in Vienna where Asperger practiced medicine, the treatment of special and difficult children was based on a combination of education and therapy. Somewhat surprisingly, however, his work was not influenced by the leading authorities of psychoanalysis of the day. He found that the methods employed by stellar figures such as Freud and Adler were unsuitable for his children, and preferred to treat them with the pervading ethos of sympathy and rehabilitation. His clinic provided lessons, speech therapy, music and exercise. The overarching approach was governed by a strong and willful desire to help and understand these troubled, different children. His ward was situated in the department of pediatric medicine, not psychiatry. He fully believed that the root cause of this condition in his children, as noted above, was biological or organic, and that this alone could account for their problems. Kanner's famous clinic at Johns Hopkins School of Medicine, on the other hand, was located within the pediatric department in the unit of psychiatry.

A Sad State of Affairs

It might be noted here that the diagnosis of schizophrenia has been used in the past to describe what we now understand as autistic behaviors. The diagnosis of schizophrenia can be mistakenly applied to persons with high functioning autism; as one pediatrician explained to me, this error can unfortunately result in an individual with autism being locked away in a mental institution or jail, which will be addressed in later chapters. In fact, estimates suggest that about 10% of any incarcerated population may be suffering from an autistic syndrome diagnosis.

Sadly, in either setting, this misdiagnosis and institutional placement leads to a downward spiral resulting in degradation, isolation, and lifelong stigmatization. In my own family, the decision to assume custody of our son was influenced by this potential lifelong threat and the fear of either incarceration or institutionalization.

Odd patterns of behavior by AS adults, such as talking to oneself or staring at strangers, can be easily misinterpreted as psychopathic by an uninformed person or an untrained member of the police or other authority figures. Psychopathic behaviors in the clinical sense of the definition may include antisocial behaviors such as a complete disregard for acceptable social norms. AS sufferers, on the other hand, may not be aware of what defines socially acceptable behaviors and rather than rebelling against social norms, appear to be disinterested or incapable of even understanding what those norms are. Absolute narcissism and mood oscillations are also included in the list of psychopathic behaviors. External stimuli (e.g., loud noises, flashing lights and touch) may evoke responses such as facial grimaces, flapping or withdrawal in AS persons, but neither anger nor violence. Psychosis, on the other hand, is a symptom of mental illness such as schizophrenia, and is characterized by radical personality changes and a distorted or nonexistent sense of objective reality. The personality of Asperger syndrome individuals appears to be predictable, steady, and stable. Their objective reality is characterized by a lack of theory of mind, according to Baron-Cohen's definition, rather than a distortion or misinterpretation of objective reality.

Dr. Digby Tantam, a British psychiatrist and one of the world's leading authorities on autism spectrum disorder and Asperger syndrome, suggests that the notion of Asperger people being the victims of bullying is a result of others sensing that this person is different and unable to conform to their expectations. Not quite fitting in is the source of emotional difficulties especially among the adult AS population. This is often due to a cumulative effect of being the victim of a lifetime of bullying even among family members who do not understand and may be embarrassed by noticeably odd behaviors such as inappropriate dress or social ineptness. It is very important to inform family members, teachers and others close to our children that although they may observe unusual, threatening or strange behavior, this unusual conduct is neither dangerous nor psychopathic. Rather than viewing this population as perpetrators of crime or violence, they are, regrettably, often the victims of abuse and bullying.

An Unfounded Theory about Vaccinations

Today we regard theories about inoculations as the source of childhood autism with skepticism, as these claims have been refuted over and over by experts in the field. The controversy about a causal relationship between the measles-mumps-rubella (MMR) vaccine and preservatives used in other childhood vaccines and their role in children developing autism has been ongoing since 1998. That was when Andrew Wakefield published his infamous paper in the highly regarded medical journal, *The Lancet*.

One vaccine ingredient known as thimerosal, a mercury-based preservative used to prevent contamination of multi-dose vials of vaccines, raised suspicion as a possible cause of autism but following a comprehensive scientific investigation, the Centers for Disease Control and Prevention (CDC) disproved this hypothesis. In a broad effort to reduce mercury exposure in children as a precaution before studies were completed, thimerosal was removed or reduced to trace amounts in all inoculations except for the flu vaccine. In 2011, an Institute of Medicine (IOM) report on the adverse effects of eight vaccines administered to adults and children, demonstrated that only with rare exceptions, the vaccines were very safe. A CDC study in 2013 added to this research by showing that vaccines do not cause an autism spectrum disorder. Underscoring the refutation of the argument linking autism with vaccines, in 2012, Andrew Wakefield's study in *The Lancet* was retracted and its editor, Richard Horton, stated unequivocally that Wakefield's claims in his 1998 article were completely false.

In May of the same year, Wakefield was stripped of his medical license in England, ensuring that he would never again be permitted to practice medicine in the UK. For most people interested in the subject of the causal relationship of vaccines and autism, denying a medical license to Wakefield and a total retraction of his claims, followed by intensive research for several years afterwards, put an end to this controversial subject.

I am not certain why some parents still embrace the causal claim of autism and vaccinations even after refutation by top medical and scientific experts, but perhaps it is their earnest effort to try to understand, accept and come to terms with this unfortunate condition. Blame, guilt and ignorance are just part of the parents' discourse who are frantically trying to understand the consequences of an AS diagnosis. I understand this fully as I, also, have searched and searched for answers and explanations where none existed.

Ineffective Therapeutic Approaches

Though I cannot speak for other parents, I would hazard a guess that medications and therapy are used as a first line of defense when their children display behavioral issues such as I have described earlier. The traditional approach just does not seem to fit and we must patiently but persistently seek other ways to deal with the upsetting, baffling and strange behaviors of our adult children. I am the first to admit that this is not an easy task, but I also believe that with time, perspective and support, we can get through many difficult, albeit predictable, periods.

Again, I must remind myself that this is a relatively new diagnosis and as such, requires more time, research and empirical studies to determine the most suitable type of remediation or rehabilitation. I support the approach which endorses counseling to help the family unit deal with the challenges it must face.

Over the past 15-20 years, we have been consulting with a British-trained psychiatrist who also believes that treating those diagnosed with AS does not warrant either intensive psychotherapy or conventional medications that are generally effective with schizophrenics. Dr. Catherine Lord, a licensed clinical psychologist specializing in diagnosis and treatment of children on the autistic spectrum, has pointed out that there is no biological treatment for AS because no adequate biomarkers have been identified to date. Her work at the Center for Autism involves continued research applying longitudinal studies. As a founding director of the Center for Autism and the Developing Brain (CADR) at the well-established NY Presbyterian Hospital, Weill Cornell Medicine and the Columbia University College of Physicians and Surgeons, she has been an outspoken advocate of early interventions. In spite of this, Lord also acknowledges that taking action at a younger age does not necessarily guarantee behavioral changes nor does the scope of the intervention promise a good outcome. Too many factors are still so unknown, she claims, to be able to guarantee families that their autistic child will reach a reasonably acceptable level of functionality in later years, especially those individuals who are non-verbal.

Throughout the years, I have realized that turning to treatment therapies including traditional psychotherapy or psychiatric medications is irrelevant given our son's condition. The issue, however, of Cognitive Behavioral Therapy or CBT as an approach which might prove to be effective, remains a more promising therapeutic method but there are a limited number of certified, qualified, and respected professionals willing and able to take on a client who has been diagnosed on the spectrum. That, unfortunately, has been our experience. Changing a behavioral pattern which has been so ingrained for so many years as is the case with our 40+ son, is a challenge and I am uncertain whether the effort, energy and resources required to identify, hire and monitor the CBT therapist is in fact worth the effort. I am still not convinced nor am I aware of any research data which clearly identifies a positive change as a result of applying CBT methods to the autistic adult. Because I am skeptical, however, I would nonetheless urge parents to find the most suitable professional who might apply some tenets to prompt their child to modify his or her behaviors, which are frequently so complicated and so strange.

Current Developments and Cautious Optimism

Environmental, medical and neurobiological variables are of great interest in the field of current autism studies. And for very good reason. Moving forward with impressive commitments of resources, scientists and scholars are conducting sophisticated research in brain development by applying scientifically-established criteria that is analyzed through powerful magnetic imaging, while geneticists advance theories of familial and biological connections amongst persons diagnosed on the spectrum. It is not at all unusual, for example, for pregnant women here in Israel, to be strongly encouraged to undergo a battery of state-financed and supported blood, genetic and other noninvasive tests even before amniocentesis is performed. If a woman mentions during prenatal counseling sessions that there is an immediate family member diagnosed with ASD, she is referred to the local geneticist to begin testing for conditions such as Fragile X that could indicate a tendency toward disabilities, including ASD. Interestingly, we cannot yet pinpoint biomarkers as evidence of an autism spectrum disorder; thus, much funding for research, time and effort is poured into trying to identify underlying neurobiological conditions with the potential of marking an autism spectrum disorder.

The Simons Foundation Autism Research Initiative (SFARI) has as its mission to improve the understanding, diagnosis and treatment of autism spectrum disorders by funding innovative research projects. Established in 2003, SFARI is a scientific initiative within the Simons Foundation programs. With an annual budget of about $75 million, it supports over 250 investigators and since its launch, has provided or committed more than $380 million in external research support. In order to sustain the drive for more research across all areas of autism science, it has created and supported resources for scientists and an impressive platform for ongoing data collection and analysis.

Simon Baron-Cohen, professor of developmental psychopathology at the University of Cambridge, is credited with a key concept in autism research called Theory of Mind—that people with autism experience severe difficulties understanding and interpreting the actions and intentions of others. He has had a major influence on research and challenged the notion that Asperger syndrome and autism should be merged under one diagnosis. Baron-Cohen still remains a primary critic of this decision taken in the recent publication of the DSM-V. He suggested that not enough studies have been conducted comparing AS to other types of autism, and to claim that there is no difference between them is a premature conclusion. Baron–Cohen was quick to dismiss the notion of autism as a mental illness; rather he considers it as both a disability and a difference in relation to social functioning and adaptation to change. He was intrigued by the apparent disconnect between intelligence and social skills, and he explored this phenomenon under the supervision of the pioneering autism researcher, Uta Frith.

A recent study summarized by Sarah DeWeerdt (2015) paints a somewhat bleak but realistic picture of treatment and intervention choices. This new report covers studies from the '80s through 2012, representing the largest analysis of autism therapies to date and the first one for adults on the autism spectrum. Of the nearly 400 studies which had been reviewed, only 7% focused on the adult population. The topic of adults on the spectrum did not even appear in the literature until close to the 1990s. The report concluded that behavioral interventions such as helping an individual on the spectrum to better communicate his or her needs, or prompting someone to take a particular action, is the only established and recognized treatment to date. Other interventions such as vocational training are seen as promising, along with social skills training and sex education. The accessibility of suitable interventions for the adult ASD population remain elusive, as resources are limited, if available at all, in a given community.

The A.J. Drexel Autism Institute is a multidisciplinary university-based research center focused on a public health approach to autism spectrum disorders. Located in Drexel University in Philadelphia, it is comprised of areas which support autism spectrum disorder research initiatives throughout the university. It is the first research-oriented organization dedicated to bringing a public health perspective to the challenges presented with an autism spectrum diagnosis. In April, 2015 Drexel University researchers published a paper with their findings that one-quarter of young adults on the spectrum do not receive any services whatsoever.

Current research strives to uncover the cause of autism, to look at the brain development *in vitro* and after birth, including those early formative years. For example, an article in *Yale News*, April, 2013, presented research suggesting that the risk of autism in families with children diagnosed on the spectrum may be spotted in abnormal placentas at birth. This finding may hold some important clues for ideal interventions during the first year of life, rather than at age three or four when diagnosis is usually given.

I remain fascinated by Dr. Asperger's working assumption that there is an organic or neurological basis to this condition. If the validity of this hypothesis can be proven, then it must drive further research, education, resources and training. It seems to me that empathy for the AS person, coupled with varied but continuous intensive rehabilitation strategies (as Asperger himself indicated nearly 75 years earlier), remain best practices in guiding our adult children through life's challenges.

Both Kanner and Asperger describe language development as signs pointing to a disturbance which may be present from birth. In a webinar presented in April, 2015 for the Simons Foundation Autism Research Initiative, Helen Tager-Flusberg described the "enormous heterogeneity" in the linguistic abilities of persons with autism, ranging from superior skills to total lack of spoken language. As the Director of the Center for Autism Research Excellence, located in Boston University, she stated that the primary aims of the center are to advance scientific knowledge about language and social communication impairments in ASD and related disturbances. In collaboration with MIT, her research compares autism and specific language impairment in MRI and behavioral studies with adolescents and children. She advocates developing interventions which may address communication challenges discovered by her teammates. Her studies using brain imaging suggest that a significant correlation exists between autism and reading disabilities, and she has found that good linguistic skills are a reliable means of predicting better outcomes for people on the spectrum. Assuming that this is the case, I think we can derive some comfort from her suggestion, as above average and even superior linguistic skills is one hallmark of an AS adult.

A new Norwegian study, however, published online in June, 2015 in the *Journal of Autism and Developmental Disorders* suggests that persons diagnosed with pervasive developmental disorders, that are not otherwise specified (PDD-NOS), are no more likely to marry or hold down a job than those with more disabling forms of autism. One recent study, in fact, notes that the divorce rate among the AS adult population exceeds 80%.

The popularity of the fictional account of a scientist afflicted with AS, *The Rosie Project*, implies that the common notion that this population is unsuitable for marriage in the traditional sense may be misleading. Though the book is well-written and has received a very positive response across the globe, the basic premise, i.e., that an AS adult is capable of major life changes, may be illusory. While entertaining and even at times humorous, it appears far-fetched. On the other hand, so little is known about the living situations of those with AS that perhaps the author, Graeme Simsion, provides us with insights, optimism and a glimmer of hope that our kids can in fact, lead productive and normal lives as understood today. Only time will tell if his fictional account parallels reality in the twenty-first century. When interviewed about his book and asked how he understood so well the mind and behaviors of an AS person, he commented that he had spent many of his adult working years in the information technology sector. In that context, he became well-acquainted with many colleagues whose mind sets, behaviors and actions fit his main protagonist, who was a professor in the field of genetics.

A Rocky Road

In a 2011 article, Deborah Rudacille noted that contrary to popular assumptions, people diagnosed with mild forms of autism do not fare better in life than those with a more severe form of autism. In fact, she suggests that even those who possess relatively strong language abilities and higher intelligence struggle to fit into society because of their problems with social and communication skills.

Anne Myhre, associate professor of mental health at the University of Oslo in Norway observed as well that high intellectual and linguistic skills cannot compensate for the profound difficulties in both communication and social abilities, a conclusion which appears to support the therapeutic approach noted by DeWeedt which focuses on behavior.

After all, it was Hans Asperger who noted that his children often used language in very clever ways, such as invented words, and that these children spoke more like grown-ups. He highlighted oddities of non-verbal communication such as eye contact, gazing and staring, bodily gestures, facial expressions, posture and clumsiness. He also reported obsessive collecting of objects which today we recognize as typical of autistic behavior. Hoarding as a diagnosis on the obsessive compulsive scale is ruled out as inaccurate, as hoarding among the population with a neurological disturbance is a non-entity. Intriguing, but often contradictory, research indicates that in their later years, AS persons do seem to suffer from psychiatric conditions such as depression beyond their population representative rate and in fact, over 60% of this AS population harbors suicidal thoughts. The rate of psychiatric disorders among the aging adult AS population, however, remains inconclusive.

Asperger noted that his children often displayed serious attention deficits and learning disabilities not unlike the suggestion made by Tager-Flusberg, of the possible existing causal correlation between autism and reading difficulties. Asperger, in fact, was an optimist who was eager to stress that his children had a good possibility of academic achievement and social adaptation. Again, his early thinking may have influenced Tager-Flusberg's theory that strong linguistic skills may predict a good outcome in individuals with high functioning autism, a position which has yet to be validated by empirical studies.

Early in our son's development, clinicians and teachers often pointed out that his high intellect did not correlate with his poor academic performance and that this gap or disconnect was a sign of a yet undiagnosed learning disability. This is a term which has often been used over the years to describe his failures in many fields, including performance on the job and social achievements. In retrospect, this is highly predictable. After all, an inability to interpret social cues and nuances is a critical disability in a work environment which often demands appropriate responses to occupational-related challenges.

Kanner also regarded language development and usage as a key marker in the diagnosis of autism spectrum disorders. However, Kanner's prototype was a child with a more severe communication disorder and the inability to generalize meaning from word sounds. Kanner's cases are very well known and generally include children who do not talk at all or who merely parrot speech. In fact, Kanner's descriptions of autistic behavior are so well documented and studied that, when in 1998 we first received our son's Asperger syndrome diagnosis, the Harvard-trained psychologist with whom he had been working for many years was shocked. Since this diagnosis was finally determined in the late nineties, it is certainly understandable that the notion that he suffered from an autism spectrum disorder was not ever considered.

Actually, there have been times when I thought that the psychologist's ignorance of this diagnosis may not have been so terrible. After all, he believed in our son's ability to readjust to life back in the US and was instrumental in helping him prepare for college. Given his intellectual skills, his excellent command of English and his high motivation to return to his native country, it seemed like a reasonable decision. We felt certain that his academic potential trumped his awkward social and communication behaviors, and that with exposure to college peers he could develop a social network which he had lacked while living in Israel. It never occurred to us that his social ineptness and limited non-verbal skills, in fact, would be the yardstick by which we identified Asperger syndrome. Verbal communication, after all, is driven by social interactions and not only by intellectual proclivities.

Chapter 2

Contradictions, Controversy and Conundrums

What Might Make the Difference

The degree of rehabilitation, adaptability and accommodation, in my opinion, is crucial in measuring personal accomplishments and achievements among the AS population. These factors are what make the difference in those with AS who have achieved notable success in their lives. Inspiring examples are Stephen Shore and Temple Grandin, both of whom are publicly identified as persons on the autistic spectrum.

Stephen Shore, an international consultant on issues related to the autism spectrum and himself affected by AS, was nonverbal until the age of four. His parents were advised to institutionalize him at a young age. He completed his doctoral degree in special education at Boston University in 2008, and is an accomplished speaker, writer, and author. His lectures and presentations are filled with humorous insights and anecdotes about coping as an adult with Asperger syndrome. He spoke at a conference for the International Center for Autism Research and Education, ICARE4 Autism, International Autism Conference in Jerusalem, August, 2012, which I attended, and I had the privilege to host him and his wife, an accomplished musician, at my home. My son came over to join us for dinner and to take part in this special opportunity to meet the couple. After Dr. Shore and his wife left, my son commented that it must be very challenging for him to teach and interact with students on the college level, as he did not make eye contact while speaking, answered questions indirectly and out of sequence, and appeared to be socially very aloof!

Another famous personality is Temple Grandin, born in 1947, who is a world-renowned autism spectrum spokesperson and advocate, as well as a consultant to the livestock industry on animal behavior. Like Shore, she is also a full professor, but she teaches in the department of animal science at Colorado State University. She is one of the first individuals affected by autism willing to share her story with the public, which has made her a celebrity. A widely acclaimed author and speaker, in 2010, Grandin was listed in the "Heroes" category in *Time Magazine 100*, an annual compilation of the 100 most influential people in the world. Like Shore, she was diagnosed at age two as brain-damaged and her family was advised to institutionalize her. Her formal diagnosis of ASD was made in the late '80s when Grandin was in her mid-forties. Temple Grandin encourages early interventions to address autism tendencies, supportive teachers, and engaging professionals trained in Applied Behavioral Analysis (ABA) to provide ongoing therapy. Although she has been criticized for trivializing some negative aspects of autism, she is a highly regarded lecturer, public speaker and advocate for autism causes. In addition, she has authored many books on the subject of her life with ASD and is the inventor of the "hug box" or squeeze box to calm hypersensitive humans, based on a similar device she designed to alleviate distressed cattle.

To date, little information is available about what makes this difference between those who achieve a high degree of professional success and less-fortunate others, whose lives remain challenged by the autistic spectrum diagnosis. I would suggest that it depends on a combination of many identifiable factors such as a favorable environment, familial sympathy and acceptance, supportive and kind teachers, strong linguistic abilities, intellectual capacity, motivation, determination, and a pleasant and appealing disposition, among other positive traits. Furthermore, acceptance of one's limitations and handicaps is an important hallmark of personal growth and development. When our son was living in the US, for example, he excelled in college, but when faced with the challenges of functioning as a productive member in the adult working community, was less successful, as scarce support was available to him in his immediate environment. He was living all alone, far away from family, and frustrated by his inability to connect with people his age. In his situation of self-imposed solitary confinement, he was filled with anger and frustration and uncertain about his future. In fact, at one meeting we had in the Atlanta community where he resided, we were told that he came seeking support from social services as he described himself as a "homeless" young man even though he lived in an apartment complex not far from where he was working.

I remember so vividly that appointment at the social service agency. Well-meaning professionals trained in the fields of mental health and social work were unable to break the code of his strange behaviors, attitude and flat verbal expression, seemingly without affect. It was a particularly sad and poignant meeting. We were living over 6,000 miles away from our son. He did not appreciate nor accept our suggestions that he consider moving back to Israel to be near his family. He had virtually no support community, and people kept their distance from him and were bewildered by his strange ways. No wonder, then, in his mind he felt metaphorically homeless as it appeared that the world had abandoned him and he really did not have a home base.

Asperger and Kanner's Theories Revisited

I would like to recount Hans Asperger's descriptions of his children as lacking the ability to function and learn in a conventional manner causing many to find alternative, creative and rather clever ways to navigate through their worlds. Rather than automatically relating to this condition as negative and disabling, he chose to see his wards as different yet with potential, stubborn but insistent on doing the right thing, viewed as menacing to those unfamiliar with the physical characteristics of the AS person, but not unkind.

To suggest that they did not have the same need for love, warmth, support and social interactions was wrong. According to Asperger, though they were unable to express or demonstrate such needs, AS individuals sought very human contact, just like any other population. Their manner of expression was different and confusing but these strong emotional needs are ever present in all of them. Here I would like to refute the patently incorrect notion that AS persons need less love or support or a network of friends. Although it often appeared to us that our son rejected our efforts to reach out and show affection and warmth, in fact, it was exactly what he needed during his early adult years. Somehow we thought that as he grew more detached from us, his nuclear family, this was also a way of establishing emotional distance which he felt was necessary in order to gain his independence.

Nothing could be further from the truth. While he seemed disinterested in us, angry and even bothered by what we thought he construed as interfering with his life, he desperately needed our full acceptance, love and support. How happy and relieved we were, therefore, when we received his phone call in which he asked us if it would be okay to move back into our home in Israel.

In his "Autistic Psychopathy in Childhood" article Asperger focused exclusively on his children, as this diagnosis had not yet been deemed a suitable one for the adults. In the introduction, he comments that the children and their case histories which he presents in the article share a "fundamental disturbance" which affects their entire behavior. However, this disorder, while profoundly affecting their social integration, may lead later in life to outstanding achievements, provided they receive exceptional educational treatment, which we can infer he developed and instituted in his own clinic. He further claims that despite their handicapping condition, they can fulfill roles in the community if given love, guidance and understanding. How basic this notion is to our understanding today of those suffering from Asperger syndrome!

It is fascinating to read Asperger's descriptions of his prototypical cases, and to try to imagine them. There is Fritz, a young man who never did what he was told, who was suffering from a severe impairment in social integration and conduct disorders. And Ernst K., who at age seven had exceptionally good speech, but was unable to get along with other children his age. He was constantly arguing with his teacher and though bright, failed in school academics. And Hellmuth L., who learned to speak relatively quickly, and when he was still a toddler, spoke like an adult.

Asperger stated that the aim of his paper was to report on a yet undeclared, unnamed personality disorder that manifested itself in childhood. But, toward the end of his seminal piece, he expressed a desire to go beyond this aim and to think about what lies ahead for this population, and what might be their potential value to society. It is at this point that we can begin to really appreciate Hans Asperger's contribution to understanding the AS adult. He observed that while social integration of these autistic people may be extremely difficult, if not impossible due to their severely impaired adaption to the social environment, this prediction applies to only a minority of cases, especially those with both autism and mental retardation.

For intellectually intact autistic persons, and in particular, those with an above average IQ, Asperger noted that their work performance could be excellent, and that could then lead to better social integration. He provided case histories to demonstrate the truth of this claim including highly regarded professors in the fields of mathematics, music and astronomy. It was their persistent and single-minded interest in these fields which ultimately led them to high academic achievements.

Asperger, fortunately, was able to observe several of his children over a time span of thirty years. In a web site I recently visited, the claim was made that such well-known people as Bill Gates and Susan Boyle may have AS, and perhaps Mozart and Einstein did too. It is an intriguing notion, though perhaps a bit far-fetched, to place undiagnosed but highly successful, somewhat different and popular individuals together under an AS category.

Autistic people, Asperger declared, do have their place in the social community and they are even capable of development and adjustment. We have the right, he stated, to speak out for our children with the "whole force of our personality." Whatever was to become of these autistic children described by his case studies awaited comprehensive study which would examine not only the biological and genetic basis, but look beyond childhood at adult development. And so, it appears that Asperger's call for future study and research is exactly where we are today, nearly 70 years after the publication of his groundbreaking paper.

Taking Kanner's descriptions of autistic children as a starting point, Lorna Wing writes (forty years later) that although there are differences in the relationship between Kanner and Asperger's descriptors of those on the autistic spectrum, they appear to have more in common and can be seen as falling within the spectrum of social impairment, differing in cognitive, language and motor functions. Kanner's classic autistic child has generally delayed and deviant language development as well as severe social impairment. Those with typical Asperger syndrome, high functioning autism, on the other hand, have good, early language development coupled with inappropriate social interactions and poor gross motor coordination as shown in posture and gait. The more able children categorized by Kanner, Wing states, might possibly develop characteristics of persons with AS and become indistinguishable from them in adult life. Though the two syndromes may blend into one another, she believes that there should be no reason not to consider Asperger syndrome as part of the autistic spectrum. Furthermore, Wing points out, impairment of social skills, including communication and interactions, has a profound effect on the development of the whole person and on the chances of that person to become an independent, productive and married adult.

Dr. Wing, a practicing psychiatrist in London, was also the mother of a daughter named Susie who had been diagnosed with Kanner classic autism in the mid-1950s. At that time, such a diagnosis was met with two observations: the autistic child was the natural outcome of the "refrigerator Mother" profile as described and accepted by the scientific community and encouraged by Bruno Bettelheim in his seminal book *The Empty Fortress,* and the only reasonable response to raising such an impaired child was institutionalization.

Wing relied on her own professional training to keep Susie out of an institution while, at the same time, she switched her research focus to delve into child psychiatry. Dr. Wing's persistence in examining and redefining the diagnosis of autism resulted in an acceptance of two distinct categories in the 1987 version of the DSM. The first one, which was linked to Kanner's classic definition, was called an autistic disorder. The second was a more broadly defined label, which could appropriately be described as a spectrum. Dr. Wing single-handedly defined a more blurred set of characteristics, and in so doing, introduced the world to what we know today as Asperger syndrome.

As Asperger noted in his 1944 article, while there are some exceptional people who have attained international fame and success, for example, Stephen Shore and Temple Grandin, the majority of individuals with this diagnosis are in need of constant guidance and supervision throughout their life span.

As the high functioning autism population begins to mature, we are faced with issues, questions and concerns relevant to an aging population. These areas will be further explored in this book, but for now I will turn to our son's early years, especially in light of what we now understand to be traits common among the autistic spectrum children. Since much current research focuses on the diagnostic criteria of children on the spectrum, I would like to review some of this research and how it is reflected in our son's later AS diagnosis.

Taking into account the chronology and history of Asperger syndrome, my son (who was born in 1974) was only seven years old when Dr. Wing's publication caught the attention of those in the field of autism. It took many more years, over a decade, until the diagnosis and its implications were generally understood. In fact, only in the early years of the '90s was the term and subsequent diagnosis beginning to be of interest to psychologists, psychiatrists, pediatricians and of course, parents.

Confusion and Contradictions

There is such abundance of opinions and ideas swirling about related to children on the spectrum that I fear we may have lost our way as we futilely tried to unravel the obscure world of the autistic in both childhood and adulthood. As with many emerging discoveries, in an effort to categorize, conceptualize and more precisely define and understand just what constitutes an AS diagnosis, we can drown in the plethora of information readily available today thanks to the sophistication of technology and of course, a growing industry and interest in the field of autism.

It is my belief that some basic misunderstandings need to be rectified in discussions on AS from a clinical perspective as defined by Dr. Asperger, and the classical autism diagnosis according to Leo Kanner. This erroneous thinking is due to both a lack of empirical evidence and research, and the rush toward trying to cope with a perceived increase in the numbers of children as well as adults diagnosed on the spectrum. Recent data suggests that approximately 1 in 68 children in the US will receive the diagnosis of autism spectrum disorder while in Great Britain the generally accepted numbers are 1 in 200. Much debate and discussions ensue even today about the actual statistics, reporting systems, rigor in data collection, and evidence-based descriptive categories.

A recent study cited by the SFARI research think tank suggests that the notion that there is an "epidemic" of persons diagnosed with autism raises certain questions. Rachel Nuwer, summarizing details of a Swedish study in her June 12, 2015 report, quotes the findings published three months earlier in the *British Medical Journal* as support for the theory that autism's rise likely stems from a greater awareness today of the disorder. The US government, keeping track since 2000 of the prevalence of the disorder, provides data indicating that the incidence of an autism diagnosis has nearly doubled over the last decade, raising alarm about an autistic epidemic. Christopher Gillberg, the lead researcher in the Swedish study, and the head of the Gillberg Neuropsychiatry Center at the University of Gothenburg in Sweden makes an interesting point. He suggests that while there has been a surge of resources spent on trying to identify the root cause of autism, the findings in the study conducted with an impressive pool of more than one million Swedish children, indicate that what has increased is actually people's awareness of autism and the fact that the diagnosis is being made at all.

While qualitative evidence is obviously significant, ascertaining the precise numbers affected in any population is far less important than accepting the notion that such a diagnosis does exist, and that it is a childhood disorder with lifelong implications. To add to the confusion about the numbers and criteria regarding the diagnosis and treatment of those on the spectrum, recent studies suggest that the notion that there is an epidemic is questionable, given the readily accessible diagnostic and research tools. In addition, this concept is being challenged by the vast resources provided by numerous organizations, non-profits and research-oriented initiatives.

In August 2015, the decision was made not to support universal screening for an autism diagnosis in very young children. Though it was a surprise to some, others agreed with the verdict for a variety of seemingly reasonable arguments.

Essentially, the timing and types of diagnostic tools for autism screening, it was implied, should best be left to the pediatrician and the family. This decision, to a certain extent, reflects the uncertainty in the field about just how valid and useful very early screening might be, given the range of diagnostic criteria and tools currently available. It did not rule out screening nor did it question its appropriateness, but merely suggested that its use be more narrowly applied.

In an interesting article by Mark Johnson, however, the author claimed that early adaptation as a neurological process may be responsible for what we refer to as characteristics of those on the spectrum. To illustrate, he explains that the young child's withdrawal from the social world may be a reasonable adaptive response, considering the difficulties experienced in processing social cues and interactions. Johnson goes on to suggest that some characteristic behavioral traits of those on the spectrum may be a reflection of whole brain adaptation, not necessarily a product of ongoing brain pathology. As noted above, screening at too early an age may be misleading, for it can find what appears to be pathology, but in actuality is an adaptation in progress. He cites another example to give credibility to his theory: a narrow focus of attention may be a good adaptive strategy for a brain struggling to process large quantities of information.

This seems to support the conclusions of a research initiative in Denmark made in 2015 that the rise of an autism spectrum disorder may be attributable to changes in how doctors diagnose the disorder rather than an actual epidemic. Furthermore, David Mandell, associate professor of psychiatry and pediatrics at the University of Pennsylvania, opined that the authors of the Swedish study probably present the most up-to-date information regarding whether or not autism symptoms have actually increased over time. He agrees with the findings in the Swedish study that the symptoms have not done so.

Diagnosis: A Blurry World

And so, at what age precisely can a child receive the diagnosis of autism spectrum disorder? It goes to follow that the answer to this question raises a whole host of other issues and questions. In truth, the definitive, chronological age of diagnosis seems less important than engaging the family in understanding, accepting, and coming to terms with the reality of the world of interventions and treatments. It is filled with meetings, conferences, sessions with speech therapists, occupational therapists, educational counselors, clinicians, psychological therapists, and the list goes on and on. Actually, the parent advocating on behalf of the disabled child can become sucked into a full time, overwhelming and exhausting cycle. Scheduling the next appointment, while tending to the needs of other family members, was extremely challenging for me. But it was also energizing as I sought out others in the community whose child-rearing experiences were similar to my own.

Given a spectrum diagnosis, some of the key issues which intrigue me personally are the following: the prediction of future adaptability, effectiveness of early intervention strategies, and integration into the social world. I would also like to consider new diagnostic approaches, discussions about how some children outgrow the diagnosis while others remain autistic, and the ways in which early identification may either help or hinder educational opportunities for those on the spectrum.

Let me begin by examining some of the research on early AS diagnosis which may go beyond Dr. Asperger's observations as presented in my last chapter. This is not an effort on my part to repudiate, question or refute Dr. Asperger's research, but merely my own personal striving to comprehend how cues and nuances of the very young child may signal even at a tender age that this youngster either has a tendency toward AS or is in fact, suffering from it. Just to remind you, Hans Asperger claimed that the condition he described as childhood psychopathy was rooted in a neurobiological disturbance which then may be exacerbated by environmental factors. Clearly, he did not have at his disposal tools to isolate and explain any hereditary manifestation, an exciting research area which today dominates many studies on the genetic causes of autism.

Are the brains of those on the spectrum and with an AS diagnosis, in some describable way, different from the normal brain? Can MRI and neurological imaging help us to isolate and understand these variations? In a study quoted in *Science Daily*, July, 2013 by BioMed Central Ltd (Duffy, Shankardass, McAnulty and Als) entitled "The relationship of Aspergers's syndrome to autism—A preliminary EEG coherence study," the authors suggest that children with Asperger's syndrome have different electroencephalography (EEG) patterns compared to children with autism. Taking this hypothesis into account about distinctive neurophysiology, this particular study adds to the discussions on just how to classify the diagnoses of the Asperger's syndrome population.

While ASD and AS disorders are closely related, noticeable neurophysiological differences were observed in this 2013 study between the groups. Although the results are preliminary and the confirmation of these findings requires a larger replicating pool, researchers do suggest that AS can be usefully defined as a distinct entity but within the higher end of the autism curve. They go on to say that just as dyslexia is now regarded as being on the low end of the reading ability curve, so too might Asperger's syndrome fit into the ASD category.

This cutting-edge field of research is exciting because if a difference can be proven, then perhaps medications or therapies can be developed which alter or even help prevent an Asperger syndrome diagnosis. Wishful thinking? Perhaps, but I can never stop wondering if there may be something out there only waiting to be discovered which can help to alleviate some of the suffering our children experience as they attempt to enter the neurotypical adult world. Again, I must remind myself that an AS diagnosis does not necessarily signify a sentence of life without love or achievements. So much depends on how the environment in which the person is living can cope and respond to someone in their midst, whose behaviors are often weird and unpredictable, and whose conduct can be frustrating, annoying and even embarrassing to close family members.

Chapter 3

Those Bewildering Early Days

Our Personal Journey

Having been affected by Asperger syndrome, our son still struggles to accept who he is and, I believe, he will go on suffering through his bouts of anger directed at his family and caregivers. However, it is encouraging to note that the frequency and intensity of these negative reactions significantly declines as he continues to mature and gains more self-respect, self-confidence and pride in his work and community involvement. As Asperger pointed out, work achievements can be reliable markers for future successes and accomplishments.

And so I must ask these difficult questions: What were we thinking all those years when he exhibited such strange behaviors? Did we rationalize his outbursts as simply going through difficult developmental stages? Weren't we perplexed at how a sweet, good-looking son could, seemingly overnight, become an angry, argumentative, uncooperative adolescent? Of course, we did consider that the move to another country could have triggered such perceived deviant behavior but we had friends and two other children whose behaviors did not confirm our rationale and suspicions.

I have often wondered how different the life of our adult son would have been, had we only been better informed about autism spectrum disorders when he was a very young child. Obviously, it is impossible to predict the future by gazing into a crystal ball to help him actualize his potential as a mature, college educated young man. It is possible, nonetheless, though disturbing and painful, to look back in hindsight in an attempt to understand more about diagnostic criteria of those on the autism spectrum and from there, to generalize to the Asperger population. As I began writing this book, I thought that it would be helpful for me personally to understand more about the Asperger child than to consider the general diagnosis of autism in childhood. As I have mentioned earlier, my son received the AS diagnosis when he was in his twenties. I will try to frame his early years with an eye toward understanding later behavioral patterns which signaled that a tendency or a trend did in fact exist.

Now I would like to focus on trying to describe the early years of a child with AS. Let's keep in mind that the AS diagnosis is so new that labeling a young child whose social and adaptive skills, by age definition, are limited, is quite a challenge. Our son's diagnosis in early years was dyslexia and learning disabled. He was therefore, entitled to an IEP, Individualized Educational Plan, untimed test-taking, and occasionally, special support in the form of extra tutoring hours. In fact, just recently during a team meeting of professionals working with our son, we were asked if he receives any assistance in the form of Social Security benefits from the U.S. government. I was at first taken back by the question until I realized that during the time he was growing up in the States until we moved when he was age 12, he had not received the AS diagnosis which explained why he did not and will not receive any benefits.

There was never any attempt to deny or neglect his learning disabled diagnosis, but rather a concerted effort on the part of teachers and educational administrators to find the most suitable support network to help him accommodate and compensate for his disability. His diagnosis in the early 80s was sometimes looked upon with skepticism, which I think is understandable, though obviously ignorant. Hard it was, indeed, to convince those service providers that a beautiful child full of energy and a zest for life could suffer any disability. After all, he looked normal, was highly verbal, and had a pleasant disposition. Perhaps, we were told, it was not our son who had a problem, but us. In fact, at one therapy session, the educational therapist recommended that the best remedy was for the family unit would be to split to lessen family tension. The child, he contended, needed quiet and safety, not the hectic atmosphere of a family that was always engaged and somewhat loud. Again, in retrospect, while it is certainly true that having a challenged child in its midst can create tension, in fact, this very unit is so important to the well-being of the child, and also during the later transition into adulthood.

I am not suggesting that families remain intact when it is not in the best interest of any members, but to imply that it is better for a child to be raised in a single parent home for the sake and security of a disabled child seems blatantly unfair. Statistically, we now know that the rate of divorce, separation, and desertion are considerably higher among the population which has a disabled child as part of the nuclear family. But as it is often said, it takes a village to raise a child. Therefore, for a family to raise a child with a disability, it takes not only a village or township but a whole continent of caring, informed, and resourceful people.

Recently I had the pleasure of attending a benefit concert in Israel sponsored by the agency providing work and support for our son. The opening presentation by a young mother of two severely mentally and physically handicapped twin daughters was poignant, brutally honest and depressing. She described the services her daughters are currently receiving in glowing terms. She spoke with calm and ease about the transition of her girls to protected housing. Finally, after her touching descriptions of their life among those with similar disabilities, she addressed the absence of their biological father. She told her audience how painfully disappointed and unhappy she and her children felt to not share this moment with him. I sensed that on some level, she was appealing to their father, wherever he may be at that particular moment, not to forget his children and to wish for him the joy and happiness she felt at this stage in her life and the lives of her twin daughters. How profoundly sad and disturbing.

Included in the evening event was a solo singing performance by a twenty something young man who was self-described as being Asperger. He sang with abandon, chatted with the audience, and was obviously happily engaged in his performance. Other than his odd dress, nothing else set him apart from any young performer who would have come to entertain a packed auditorium. Yet, he was a resident in a protected housing unit, working in a candle-making factory, and unable to develop social contacts with others his age. He is a talented singer and has been in other performances in the community. When he climbs up on the stage, he is seemingly transformed, almost as if he momentarily breaks out of the spectrum diagnosis.

Snowflakes: No Two are Alike

In describing human interactions and behaviors, nothing is black or white, predictable or erratic, clear or blurred. We can observe certain tendencies or general patterns, but these are neither absolute nor sustainable. What may be true and accurate in our descriptions of the little Asperger child is that he or she is like a snowflake, swirling and reconfiguring itself as it drifts toward the ground. One snowflake never resembles another. Each is simple in its formation and unpredictable in its speed, changing direction and pattern and then disappearing into the warm earth never to be seen again. And so it is so like our Asperger children. While there are obvious similarities as described by Kanner and Asperger and later elaborated upon by Lorna Wing, - a silent, aloof, naïve and clumsy little person - the intensity, frequency and predictability of any of these characteristics varies in each child and over time.

In an interview conducted by Diane Rehm on National Public Radio in June, 2015, Valerie Paradis described her own childhood, adolescence and early adult years. She spoke openly about feeling different, isolated and marginalized in spite of the support of her siblings and professional therapists, and the praise she received for her academic achievements. She was diagnosed with AS at age 40 when she sought help for her son who is on the autistic spectrum. As no genetic test can definitively diagnosis the autistic spectrum condition, most often it is the observations of family members and self-description which inform the diagnosis according to Paradis. During the interview, others described the current state of treatment in the United States for the autistic spectrum adult population as inadequate and even unavailable after the legal school age. According to one speaker, when one left the public school system, it was like "falling off the cliff" for the child and family. It is estimated that in the U. S. alone, over 50,000 children officially diagnosed as being on the spectrum will enter adulthood each year. In addition, it is predicted that 4.5 million autistics on the spectrum over the next decade will graduate from high school to a situation with hardly any support or services, referred to as a "tsunami" phenomenon.

Some children display extraordinary linguistic skills while others maintain a mysterious silence. There are children who try to engage in some sort of social intercourse, albeit often in strange ways such as lecturing on their subjects of interest, while others remain distant and seemingly uninterested in any form of social engagement. Some children seem to lack empathy and any theory of mind as described earlier by Simon-Cohen, while others show intense feelings toward pets or special people in their immediate environmental orbit. In fact, our descriptions today of an Asperger child alter with time and place to the extent that what is predictable and now known, may be entirely inaccurate and untrue in a few years.

The tendency to exhibit certain behaviors is often missed as the child develops interests and engages in activities that may appear to be age appropriate. For example, as a little boy, our son was fascinated by dinosaurs and dragons. He created all types of figures with blocks and Lego which according to his descriptions and his thoughts fit the world of dinosaurs as he imagined it. During his early years, we were so excited by his intense interest in paleontology that we spent hours in museums looking at the reconstructed figures of early Man. And this interest took on special meaning as he was later fascinated by the evolution of our prehistoric ancestors from Neanderthal man to *Homo sapiens.*

In the fourth edition of the Diagnostic and Statistical Manual of Mental Disorders published in 1994, the first criteria of the AS diagnosis is the impairment in social interactions, a lack of reciprocity, and modulation of behavior. For example, during play, a child with AS can dominate or dictate the rules, and be oblivious to the wants and needs of the other playmates. Creating games and adventures were activities which did include others, but only on their terms. The AS child apparently fears an alternative game or activity which might threaten or challenge his assumptions about what is acceptable or right by his interpretation only. It is as though the child is playing in a bubble, even when the social interaction would appear at first glance to be normal play behavior. One adolescent with AS, for example, had trouble understanding how in competitions, a winning team could feel such joy and satisfaction, knowing the opponent failed and as a result felt a sense of inferiority. Our son rejected our efforts to encourage him to participate in sports. While he was strong and even physically big for his age, he could not grasp the concept of winning over others. Team playing was not something he enjoyed, and he was more drawn to activities such as playing Solitaire in order to avoid interacting with others. He could not envision himself as a member of a team but felt more comfortable following his own interests. In that sense, he appeared to be much more self-centered than selfish.

Recently on a visit to a local museum, our son was expounding upon human evolution in a loud voice, gesturing with his hands to the extent that he actually drew an audience that assumed he was a guide in the museum. He was very happy to continue his lecture even when only a few people remained. And yet, his efforts at initiating simple conversation or engaging someone in a discussion are often misguided and inappropriate. How can we teach him to use conventional language in a way which is suitable to the social situation? We have tried, continue to try and will not give up trying, though it remains unclear if this goal is fair, realistic or even attainable.

Rejection and Withdrawal

Our son had two very close friends with whom he remained in touch even after we emigrated from the US. One friend went so far as to attend his high school graduation in Israel, but was obviously confused as this person was not the one he had befriended 10 years earlier. In fact, they met up later when our son enrolled in Curry College in the Boston area and his former friend attended a prestigious university relatively close by. I recall how hurt and upset our son was when his buddy abandoned him on several social occasions and then refused his sincere effort to reach out and reestablish a friendship. Our college age son was not the one he had remembered from the early days of elementary school. This person was aloof, awkward, and socially disconnected. Could we or anyone else have seen this remarkable transformation or was it really so extraordinary? Perhaps this change was simply an extension of who our son had been in his early years but the expectations were so very different. He was, after all, still the same guy. Shy as a young seven year old but retiring as a young adult. His realm of fantasies that had been age appropriate for a 10 year old was so unbecoming for a college graduate seeking employment in a world which did little to encourage or value creative thinking. Able to speak with the authority of a learned adult on the many subjects that interested him at the age of 12 but when lecturing to those close by, such behavior was denounced as detached from reality. And relationships with girls! He was so cute with a charming smile that at an early age, aggressive little girls flirted with him while attempting to engage him in chit-chat. As a young adult, he was expelled from a local university for what was interpreted as sexual harassment, after he had made a clumsy attempt to initiate a conversation with a female lecturer while riding up several floors in an elevator.

What I wish to describe here is how perspectives can and often do inform expectations. Can a young adult engaged in what he perceives to be socially acceptable behavior be denounced or even legally prosecuted because what seemed to be correct and true at an earlier period in his life is not so in later years? We now know, for example, that the ability to accept behavioral change can confound an AS person. After all, their logic would suggest, why is a particular form of conduct at one age understood and acceptable yet at a later age, seen as strange and menacing?

Why can't the rich fantasy world of a youngster's mind be extended to the virtual realm, with an imaginary girlfriend, in his adult years? After all, the logic would suggest, what is wrong with a virtual girlfriend since the world of dragons and dungeons at an early age gave him such joy and entertainment? And dress codes. After all, wearing the same shirt and pants for weeks, though washed nightly by the mother, might predict a similar pattern of behavior in an adult. After all, logic would suggest, buying 15 of the same color, size and style of a favorite shirt is sensible to the AS person since finding a comfortable style and clothing texture presents its own challenges. It was, after all, not so simple to shop for just the right size and texture and once discovered, why change?

Recently, my son went to an Independence Day party at a local venue, and he was very pleased to see a young woman who had befriended him a few weeks earlier in his workplace. She was one of the volunteer instructors doing some tasks in an office close to his. They chatted, drank tea, and engaged in conversations which he described as pleasant and comfortable. He was so hurt and upset when he saw her at this party and rather than engaging in conversation or dancing with him, she coldly turned away and showed no desire for social contact. He simply could not understand that work place chatter was not indicative of any interest in pursuing a social relationship. As a result, he expressed frustration and pain at being scorned by her. In other words, he was simply not capable of understanding that what he perceived to be genuine interest in him was merely the kind of friendly chitchat typical of a workplace, and nothing more. His inability to separate out and respond appropriately to the role changes caused him incredible pain which later translated into reluctance to make any future attempts to connect to women. Perhaps, however, over time, he will develop social tools which may enable him to form those bonds with people that he so desperately seeks. Perhaps, over time and with more exposure, he can adapt his responses to fit the occasion. I am cautiously optimistic that with maturity, exposure and growth, he may develop essential insights and knowledge to help him navigate through the social mazes of life.

I can appreciate and understand so many of these seemingly contradictory or inexplicable behaviors, but as I now know so well, understanding and acceptance are not necessarily complimentary. Thinking in a different way, as Digby Tandem suggests, can create emotional turmoil and most people avoid any such potential and discomfiting dissonance. In fact, in the area of negotiations and conflict resolution, one of the intriguing principles is that of cognitive dissonance. People generally do not tolerate silence well and often try to fill these awkward moments with compromises and concessions, a move understood and perpetuated by a seasoned negotiator.

Tony Attwood claims in *Asperger's Syndrome: A Guide for Parents and Professionals* (1998) that the diagnosis for this disorder in children can come in two stages: first a teacher or parent uses a rating scale, and second, by means of a diagnostic assessment conducted by a professional using established criteria. In describing the diagnosis, Attwood makes the case that AS is a variant of both autism and a PDD, Pervasive Developmental Disorder and that it is a diagnosis more common than the classic Kanner autistic child. As with our son it could also be true that the AS diagnosis in a child may be included within the population that had never previously been considered autistic. Our son, as noted earlier, received the diagnosis of learning disabled but not autistic. It was only many years later when he was in his early twenties did the AS diagnosis appear to fit his behavior. In college, he worked closely with a counselor whose diagnosis was a narcissistic injury caused by his being uprooted at a young age. Only then, after college and several years of unsuccessful living alone as well as the failure to find a steady job, did we begin the official diagnostic process, for which we completed a questionnaire provided by a referral agency, and further examination and substantiation by a trained clinician.

Dr. Catherine Lord points out that the AS diagnosis is based on behavioral observations. While speaking at the Summer Institute for Autism Research in July, 2015, she poignantly summed up the family situation when she claimed that "a family will never be the same when a child is diagnosed with autism." There could be nothing truer than that.

By being unreasonable, illogical and in denial, it was not until we received the written document by the agency did I fully accept and come to terms with the Asperger syndrome, high functioning autism diagnosis. We had been through years of endless counseling, psychiatric and psychological referrals, educational assessments, and behavioral training sessions, parent support groups, and individual, family and couple counseling. Despite all that, only after I had read and fully understood the diagnosis, both in writing and well-documented by a professional staff, was I actually willing to come to terms with the reality that our son's behavior was neither sick nor deviant, but a result of a profoundly disruptive disorder, not of his choosing or his fault, and not his responsibility.

Becoming a Tiger Mom

Out of necessity and not in keeping with my naturally shy and retiring disposition, I became an aggressive, demanding and even outspoken tiger Mom, cajoling, coercing and sometimes threatening those in charge with legal actions if my son's needs were wrongfully ignored or intentionally overlooked.

I vividly recall the moment when the service providing agency here in Jerusalem called me. Since his condition was formally accepted by the ministry charged with working with the autistic community, as a young adult, my son was entitled to a range of services including work support and housing. I was stunned. Although I desperately tried to hold back my tears, the trained psychologist on the other end of the telephone no doubt sensed my shock as we agreed to meet later in the week to begin the rehabilitation process. I choose to use the word rehab very carefully as I shall explain further on. I see our son's journey as a process of ongoing rehabilitation in the classic Hans Asperger sense. Our son has a neurobiological condition which is lifelong and pervasive. His choices are informed by his diagnosis, and our commitment to helping him to manage those decisions remains, even today, our greatest challenge.

CHAPTER 4

The Bright Smiling Boy

<hr>

Preschool and Elementary School Days

My son's experience while he attended preschool in Miami, Florida was quite uneventful. He enjoyed interacting with other children, followed instructions, and was a happy, playful child. However, he did have trouble focusing and staying engaged and on task according to the preschool teachers. We signed him up for Suzuki violin lessons in an effort to bolster his ability to focus his attention over a reasonable time span. His first performance on the tiny, but polished and well-preserved violin was a source of pride and accomplishment for his family and his self-esteem. He was serious about the correct posture, finger placement, and care of his instrument. He took swimming lessons, had play dates, and enjoyed his story times just like any other child, yet there seemed to be something not quite fitting for his age which we found hard to describe. Since we had an older son with whom to compare, we saw disturbing developmental differences.

Seeking out a reputable psychologist, he was put through a series of tests to determine if he had any disability. It seemed, even at such a young age, that there was a gap between his ability and stimuli and his performance and output. We were told that there were processing issues which required professional interventions, but that some playtime activities including structured and focused play sessions, quiet times so he could integrate what had happened during the day, and reduced noise stimuli might be helpful. His hearing and his vision were checked. Reflexes seemed within the normal range, but information processing, which stimuli were received, interpreted, processed and output remained weak and below normal for his chronological age.

His environment was crammed with educational toys and books but occasionally we noticed that certain noises as well as light disturbed him to the extent that he cried until we were able to minimize these external stimuli. In fact, today discussions are under way about the connections between the lack of control mechanisms in the autistic brain which results in the child being over-stimulated and the ability of the child to filter the excessive stimuli being received.

In 2015, Alan Packer, a senior scientist at the Simons Foundation Autism Research Initiative, described the habituation process as the brain's ability to adapt over time to such stimuli as sights and sounds as possibly less rigorous and less competent among the autistic population. The sensory hypersensitivity which our son experienced even as a young child was something that we tended to forget or ignore. It was often a source of frustration and upset in his early years, triggered by bright lights, loud noise, even different smells. These stimuli might suddenly provoke an overreaction and depending on where we were at the time, result in melt downs and temper tantrums. Over time, however, he seems better able to adapt in a way which has not interfered with his normal activity, though how well he has habituated is very hard to measure. Today, for example, noisy visits with his nieces and nephews often result in his leaving the room and finding solace watching TV in a quiet place and space in our apartment. We no longer argue or question his departure but try to accept this behavior as an outcome of what we perceive as his heightened sensitivity to external stimuli. In other words, we, as a family, no longer become agitated or upset by his sudden disappearance nor do we fight it. Instead, we try to provide a comfortable space for his much needed down time.

To our delight but not surprise, the standard IQ tests demonstrated that he had above average to superior scores in verbal areas though I do not recall the exact numbers. His performance in other areas was good but again, the information processing seemed to be a big issue. We later understood that this processing deficit would eventually lead to a diagnosis of dyslexia, then to learning disabled, and ultimately the giant leap, as Stephen Shore described it: the autism spectrum bomb was dropped.

Am I suggesting that there is a continuum at work here? Frankly, I do not know the answer nor am I convinced that studies have demonstrated a clear trend in this direction. Can early childhood deficits become adult disabilities? Is it possible to draw conclusions about the future developments of a child with an early age attention deficit disorder diagnosis? I do not have answers to these questions but I do share the hopes of so many parents of children diagnosed at an early age with childhood deficits that some tentative answers, even speculative and inconclusive ones, may be beneficial in the decision-making process for their young children.

When our son was five years old, we relocated from Florida, to Rockville, Maryland where he was enrolled in a progressive, reputable, and well-established private Jewish Day School. As moving day drew near, our children participated in helping to pack up the house and their toys, throw away anything they no longer wanted, and donate used toys for others to enjoy. Here was the problem. Our son was completely incapable of making any categorical distinctions. In his mind, everything and anything which he owned was personal and valuable and he stubbornly refused to give up any of his possessions. Finally, after weeks of exhausting arguments, threats and negotiations, we agreed that he could keep everything. To the dismay of the packers and movers, even his garbage including gum wrappers, tissue paper and odd pieces of collected paper were packed up and moved to our new home. As I would later come to understand, part of this hoarding tendency is a hallmark of AS adults, tolerated to a certain degree in children, since item collection is an effort to avoid any changes in the immediate environment. We interpreted his need for collecting as an attempt to hang on to stability and predictability. Hoarding as a psychiatric clinical diagnosis, in fact, does not apply to those on the spectrum. While the result is the same, the motivation is very different indeed.

Since our son had exhibited outstanding verbal skills, he had little trouble fitting into the intellectually charged learning environment of the new school.

In fact, he appeared to be excited by the prospect of engaging in intellectually challenging activities. A problem arose when it came to learning to read and to write. He was able to learn a second language with little effort as the approach to teaching Hebrew in the curriculum of this particular school was verbal. His memory was good and his ability to imitate and produce a foreign language was strong. He seemed to be wired for the grammar of the new language and his extensive passive vocabulary was age appropriate. However, due to his difficulties in processing, we were advised that he repeat his kindergarten year to give him time to mature. I am not convinced that this was a wrong or right decision for him since repeating the year a second time did little to advance his information processing skills, so vital for learning how to read and write.

One thing I was sure about. In kindergarten, he was a friendly, happy, outgoing fella. He went to school each day with a big smile on his face and found the love and support of his professional kindergarten teacher to be a wonderful source of comfort. Not until our son was under her guidance for a few months did we learn from her that she had a disabled daughter living at home. I do not remember nor do I know if I was ever told about the extent of the little girl's disability, but this woman's compassion, acceptance and work with our son were extraordinary. Very few of his teachers since then demonstrated such outstanding inner resources and personal motivation to work with our special student.

Several incidents occurred at school that had a devastating effect on our child. One nasty teacher called him a "bump on the log" for sitting through her boring classes and not responding appropriately to her questions. My son, so happy and smiling, was crying when I picked him up from school. It took quite some time that afternoon to get him to tell me what had happened to make him cry embarrassingly in front of his school pals. I still remember the anger I felt toward anyone who could be so insensitive as to name call and bully a six-year-old child. Enraged, I returned to the school a few hours later and demanded to speak to the principal on the spot. After she calmed me down, I told her what had happened. She agreed to confront the teacher the very next day and demand an apology to our son. She was subsequently put on probation as I can only assume other little ones had been bullied by her; the following year, her contract was not renewed.

There was an earnest and successful effort made by the school to identify and meet the needs of our child. As a public school teacher myself at the time, I was very aware of the system's responsibility to accommodate his special needs. Mainstreaming was a crucial area of discussion but there was never any question about taking him out of the age-appropriate class room. In fact, he was given extra tutoring which he happily accepted and this service did not clash with outdoor play time as it was felt that he needed physical activity as much as the extra support. In a clever and nondestructive way, the system responded gently and effectively to his special needs. He had his play pals, birthday parties, and Boy Scout activities to keep him happy and engaged but this was not without major efforts on the part of the family. His necessities and happiness seemed to dominate our family discussions and often the choices we made were the direct result of his special needs. His siblings went along with our decisions with little fuss and much acceptance. In fact, it was a *modus operandi* of our family years together that what was in our son's special needs and interests was also in the best interest of the family. His brother and sister accepted his dominant role in the family with good humor, love, and grace. If there was a neighbor bully, his siblings came to his defense. He was also included in their activities and was always a cooperative family member.

Having said this, however, there were obvious tensions. For example, he and his brother had always shared a room together but as they grew older, his wants, collections, and refusal to accept certain realities resulted in angry outbursts and days of unending conflict and verbal battles. We finally took over the basement and converted it into a bedroom for our eldest son. He was also having difficulties in focusing, so family tasks took up inordinate amounts of time and patience. To make matters worse, he developed allergies requiring special care with his diet and environment, and weekly shots to protect him from his dust allergy.

Medication: Helpful or Harmful?

At the suggestion of the pediatrician and due to the teachers' reports of his fluctuating attention span, my son began taking Ritalin. The medication worked in terms of helping him to focus better and to become more manageable, but the desired results came at a very high price. Our son became socially quiet, withdrawn and apathetic, losing the keen interest in things he had previously loved like his special dinosaur collection. The outgoing friendly guy had become reclusive and sad. The teachers were satisfied and we were distraught.

He was content to remain aloof and quiet, and no longer seemed to need so much extra time from his academic environment, requiring less intervention, support or explanations from the teaching staff. He focused more on academic stimuli while understanding just as little, but at least he was quiet and easy to manage in the classroom. His drugged state was interpreted as cooperation and his former lack of attention was replaced by disinterest. His zest and enthusiasm for whatever was happening around him became aloofness. I remember so well going to a religious service one Saturday and while sitting next to our son, noticing to my chagrin how detached he was. He was not at all interested in singing or joining others his age after the service was over in a game outside and it was at that very moment that I made the decision to stop the Ritalin. After a short period of time, my son was returned to me in full gear - full of energy, questioning things teachers presented to him, verbally outspoken and a robust athlete. Did he learn as much as he might have had he continued with Ritalin? I do not know but today I realize that in the adult population, psychiatric medications for the treatment of schizophrenia are often used to treat those on the spectrum, yet they have not been proven effective.

Larry Young, director of the Silvio O. Conte Center for Oxytocin and Social Cognition at the Emory University in Atlanta, Georgia, points out that research done with the hormone oxytocin have been inconclusive. Adam Guastella, a clinical psychologist at the University of Sydney, goes further by suggesting that the biology under study is "incredibly complex". Discussions about oxytocin, the "feel good" hormone which mothers experience after giving birth, creating intimate bonds with their newborn child, have been both promising and disappointing in their efforts to demonstrate a causal relationship if administered to those on the spectrum. In studies on neuroimaging and its relevance to autism, Kevin Pelphrey warns that the contextual framework of using oxytocin in the spectrum population might be problematic for a young adult, who may seek affection and emotional affirmation, and therefore resort to unsuitable and inappropriate hugging responses. In other words, consideration must also be given to the application and result of taking any type of medications that modify behavior, a reasonable and fair precaution in my opinion.

Nonetheless, I am not suggesting that properly administered and carefully monitored medications have no role to play. In fact, when our son became an adolescent, a light sedative to be self-administered was prescribed by our pediatrician with the advice of his psychologist. He was given very clear directives about when to take his medications and as far as I knew, he never abused its usage; in fact, he reported that his social anxiety had been lessened. In his adult years, however, he continues to refuse any medications, even a light sedative which may or may not help him with his moments of uneasiness. As an adult, I respect his decision. Yet, being his mother, I do sometimes wish that the pain caused by his high levels of anxiety could be reduced if he were to take a light sedative once in a while.

Recently, research conducted by William Catterall examined the efficacy of anti-anxiety drugs in the benzodiazepine class of medications. His team conducted a five-year study and found that, in some instances, its monitored usage may be helpful. His study focused on the sodium channels initiating active potential in the excitable cells which drive the electric signals in the brain. A long standing theory, according to Catterall, posits that autism may arise from what he describes as an "imbalance of excitability and inhibition signals" in the brain. This class of drugs, he suggests, may help to restore an imbalance thus reducing anxiety.

It is an interesting theory but in my son's case, his unwillingness to take medication of any kind cancels out all hope that we have found some reasonable avenue to help him reduce his social anxiety. This is often expressed by overeating during a noisy family dinner or, as mentioned earlier, going off by himself to the solace of a quiet, isolated place. If we take him to a concert or other performance, we are always careful to try to find a seat, often in a balcony, where he can enjoy the event without interacting with others. Our consulting psychiatrist warned us against resorting to psychiatric medications under most circumstances, a warning we have heeded and taken very seriously. Our son seems to instinctively understand what is in his best interest when it comes to self-administered psychiatric drugs, though he has gone to the extreme to the degree that he refuses to take even an aspirin and has rejected one dentist's recommendation that he must have some teeth extractions. I do worry about how he will deal with medical issues as he ages. I think that this is an area that must be addressed in the future as most likely there are others on the spectrum, for reasons not completely clear to me, who are fearful and suspicious of drugs and even medical practices.

Learning to Learn

Returning to his earlier years and social conduct, I can remember enrolling him in a summer program for special needs children offered by the public school system. Feeling overwhelmed and concerned about what I perceived to be stigmatization of special needs children, I was not convinced that this class suited him. I remember feeling relieved yet curious when I saw how happy and comfortable he was with others in the classroom whose special needs were never clear to me. He was greeted with warmth and affection, accepted by children his age, and welcomed into the community school setting. He never objected to attending the program which lasted the full summer nor did he express sadness at not being with his former classmates from the other school. I was surprised but pleased that he had a positive learning experience but never regretted my insistence that he be mainstreamed while receiving support services during his parochial school years.

Since his dyslexia diagnosis persisted and eventually became an issue, I decided that he must learn to read and write in order to survive the challenges facing him ahead. One summer, he met with a wonderful learning specialist whose training and qualifications for assisting dyslexic children were outstanding. Each day we traveled back and forth to her clinic where he received intensive instructions along with positive reinforcement from her and from our family. As a unit, we took an active part in his learning, drawing symbols in sand boxes for hours, making silly sounds that were then recorded and decoded, and engaging in other learning activities designed to help our son master the codes for learning to read and write.

During this period, one of the teachers in his school raised serious doubts about his ability to ever decode sufficiently to be able to read. As a result, I returned to the university to renew my teaching credential, and took an excellent course in teaching young children to read. Not a preschool professional myself, I decided that I needed to learn more about the reading process. I was introduced to the writings and theoretical framework of Frank Smith, who asserted that any and all youngsters are capable of learning how to read. Smith claimed that if they did not succeed, then the problem was with the teacher and the system, not the child. It was a fascinating and somewhat controversial theory but I adopted it as my own, quoting it often to teachers who had been skeptical about my son's capacity to ever learn enough decoding to read with fluency. To our delight, he eventually became an avid reader. Even so, throughout his elementary and high school years, and even in college, he did receive some support; however, it was mostly related to timing and focusing issues.

When he got older, one of the adaptive or compensatory tools he was taught as a learning disabled college student was to chunk the information he needed to master for his courses. As pointed out by Johnson, by focusing on specific objects or interest domains, those on the spectrum may be better able to grasp a more comprehensible subset or chunk of information. Thus, by absorbing bits of information at his own pace, my son was able to integrate the information sufficiently to pass his exams with flying colors.

Unfortunately, social skills training for that age did not exist, as it was assumed that little people at play did not necessitate much mediation. Scant attention during those years was paid to children's social needs. If a child was overly aggressive, a system in place was activated to deal with the issue. However, social nuances and cues, social conduct and withdrawal were not framed as requiring intervention or retraining. The common notion back then was the child's intuition and innate need to behave with socially acceptable responses was always present and it was simply a matter of time or opportunity for him or her to express what was considered to be innate. My son was in school systems in the late 70s and early 80s; this was over thirty years since Asperger's writings about unusual children had been in place but, unfortunately, were not read in most English-speaking countries. Together with interventions for focusing, processing and decoding issues, had we only been aware of Asperger's discoveries, we would have also sought help for social skills development. And perhaps, just perhaps, we could have helped him to overcome this significant but overlooked deficit. Wishful thinking? Perhaps, but if a child can be taught compensatory skills to be able to learn to read and write at the college level, then surely social skills training could go a long way in helping the child to decode the baffling world of human interactions.

Life with an AS Family Member

Since it became apparent that the school system had overlooked providing any social skills to my son, I therefore took it upon myself to compensate for this lack in our own home environment. As any parent knows, the child-rearing journey is a complex and challenging one even under ideal circumstances, but raising a child with special needs can become an end unto itself. In other words, it is not so difficult to devote most waking hours to pondering the needs of this special child to the extent that other family and community issues become subordinate. In my case, however, because of the nature of the communities to which we belonged and the professional obligations of my family (my husband is a rabbi), I had no choice but to look beyond the needs of my child. In hindsight, and after years of introspection, I must say that perhaps these time demands on me as a mom, wife and teacher were a blessing in disguise. While often emotionally overwrought and physically exhausted, the demands on my time required that I transcend the urgent needs of my son. I was forced to make deliberate, weighty decisions in the best interest of my immediate family. Dashing from appointment to appointment, entertaining community leaders on a regular basis, and attending to the needs of my two other children, required me to step aside and look beyond the moment in order to allow myself to multitask and multifunction. I believe that both my family and I benefitted from my priority setting and time adjustments as I did my best to keep all these moving parts operating in tandem.

Bearing in mind that the diagnosis of high functioning autism basically did not exist during his childhood, we struggled during those initial years. We made frustrating attempts to comprehend his behaviors and in doing so, to make our lives and those of his siblings more normative. There were so many contradictions. For example, his behaviors at home and within the family environment often appeared normal but reactions to changes in environment or being in unfamiliar surroundings resulted in sometimes aggressive, other times, withdrawn behaviors.

It was nearly impossible to predict how he might respond. We did not change or adjust our social gatherings to take his needs into consideration, however, we could not know in advance if there would be a reaction or not and if so, the intensity or duration or consequences.

We desperately tried to carry on in as much a normative way as was possible, but needless to say, this created stress and tension within our family circle. Of course, at the time, we could not know that with his adolescence would come the social isolation and exclusion so painful and profoundly sad for an AS teenager. We never discussed our son's peculiar ways with our other two children. Since we did not have a diagnosis to frame such a discussion, we settled instead for flexibility, understanding and compromise, nearly impossible demands to put on siblings although ours seemed to develop an attitude of acceptance and family obligations. I insisted on civil discourse and behavior, though with three youngsters born only a few years apart, this demand was sometimes rather difficult to enforce.

The notion which is widely accepted today that a child can be taught and coached to understand nuances in social situations did not exist when our son was school age. Innate codes of conduct which come naturally to youngsters were simply not understood by our son. While he did not misbehave to the extent that in public he had to be punished or reprimanded by an adult, his actions did seem a bit strange. Sometimes in the middle of a board game, he would simply pick himself up and retreat to his room, paying little attention to the rules. He appeared to enjoy the playfulness of his hamsters, David and Daniel, taking comfort from the antics of his little furry friends. In a recent study, I read that these little creatures can offer such solace and friendship to those on the autistic scale that just holding or watching them may be considered an appropriate method of animal-assisted therapy. Gretchen Carlisle, a human-animal interaction specialist at the University of Missouri, has shown that while previous research focuses on how dogs are highly beneficial for children on the AS spectrum, contact with animals of any kind can help improve their social skills.

Certain social encounters, while intuited naturally by the neurotypical child, required much thought and analysis on his part. Once taught, however, he was able to exercise good judgment in somewhat similar future encounters. The sad reality, of course, was that most social encounters change over time and it was difficult, if not impossible, to predetermine what he should be taught that could be generalized to other social situations. We focused on codes of etiquette and insisted that he follow a repertoire of responses which he could learn and apply to many situations. This turned out to be a good approach. Today, as an adult, he is able to exercise fairly good judgment, so that he behaves politely in situations which are either challenging or unfamiliar to him.

Chapter 5

Growing Pains: Adolescence to Early Adulthood

Turbulent Times

Looking at the chronology of my Asperger syndrome son's development, I am struck by how major upheavals in our lives may have had a very strong and perhaps even detrimental impact on his social and cognitive development. The typical characteristics of persons with Asperger syndrome was virtually unknown during his early years from birth to preadolescence and then into adolescence and young adulthood. Fear of change, inflexibility and a social skills deficit are now understood to be hallmarks of the AS individual. On the other hand, our son would lack the intellectual and social richness that exposure to another language and culture gave him. Learning to adapt to another way of life, appreciating that others may have a distinct set of values and attitudes, and understanding that people can act differently from what he had been taught — all of this afforded him greater awareness of his own condition and identity.

Tony Attwood, a renowned writer, lecturer, and mental health expert who specializes in AS, has written extensively about the different challenges and life stages of those who have been diagnosed with AS. Born and educated in Britain and living in Australia, Attwood expresses himself eloquently as both a practicing psychologist and as an involved father of a son on the spectrum. For those diagnosed with AS according to the DSM-5, Level 1 is the term used to identify those on the spectrum which is different from the classic Kanner diagnosis. In the most recent DSM publication, it was shown that the AS diagnosis merged into the category of autism spectrum disorder. Addressing issues for those with AS, Attwood singles out adolescence as the most trying and difficult time in the developmental stage of the youngster, who is transitioning from puberty into adulthood. Along with the standard criteria used to specify an ASD, he designates a list of major issues that teenagers confront: physical changes, learning styles, sexuality and friendships, controlling emotions, and thoughts about future plans such as university or employment.

Adolescents naturally enjoy exchanging bits and pieces of information about those of the opposite sex with their friends, and are curious about sharing codes of behavior in different situations. Yet this rarely happens in an individual with high functioning autism. As the failure to socialize and experience meaningful interactions with others becomes increasingly pronounced and stressful, the teenage years for those who suffer with AS become more and more complex. They are often unable to successfully initiate or maintain pleasant conversations, or to communicate emotions and engage in reciprocal activities. It would seem that neurotypical teenagers would also thrive on the opportunity to reach out, to share their feelings and experiences with their peers, yet they are often inhibited from doing so. To illustrate, during his three years as a student at the excellent American School in Israel, our son never once had a friend over. Similarly, he was never invited to anyone's home for any occasion, nor did he participate in the popular disco dances and junior and senior proms. He didn't show much interest in girls and he never went out on a date. It was as though that part of his life was unimportant and irrelevant. We interpreted this lack of social engagement with peers as a consequence of his living outside of the community where the school was located. Since he commuted many hours each way just to get to school each day, we rationalized that he was simply too exhausted to bother with social activities. In hindsight, we now understand that this aversion to any experiences which had a social component was a result of his AS condition and not related to how far his residence was from his school.

The Pain of Rejection

Our son, who was sweet and very good looking did, however, become interested in our daughter's friend who frequently visited our home. When he began to develop her acquaintance, both she and our daughter were pleased. One day, however, in an innocent act that was perceived as aggression, he frightened our daughter's friend to the point that she said she would no longer feel comfortable coming over to visit if he were there.

As Attwood notes, moving along the intimacy continuum from acquaintance to friend, and then to boyfriend or girlfriend, involves a multifaceted repertoire, which includes the art of flirting, reading the signals of mutual attraction, and understanding what it means to go out on a date. Our son, like most people with high functioning autism, simply lacked the intuition required for healthy relationship building. Our daughter's friend was offended by his seemingly aggressive behavior as his actions were inappropriate and he never shared with her his feelings or attempted to display any affection toward her. He simply followed what he felt were the rules for the right way to engage in a relationship. Conversational exchanges, going out on dates, subtle expressions of affection and any other signs that he considered her as a potential girlfriend were not on his Asperger radar screen. The know-how to cultivate a mutually caring relationship with a girl was not instinctive to him, as he lacked the age-appropriate skills in the pragmatics of language and relationship building.

After this agonizing episode, our son felt rejected and sad. His sister gently reprimanded him about his behavior but he neither accepted nor understood his role and responsibility for what happened. Instead, his response to this painful experience was to entirely cut himself off from any possibility of ever having a girlfriend. He became more reclusive and withdrawn, and completely avoided social engagements with his peers. He continued to feel unwanted, humiliated and ridiculed, which seemed to describe his socially and emotionally empty teenage years.

While he did receive plenty of academic support through the outstanding services provided by this high school, the development of social skills, interpersonal relationships, and protocol were never addressed, nor was this the expectation. He approached and went through adolescence in the late 80s and early 90s, a time when the topics of ASD and AS were just beginning to interest educators and parents. Our son was born too early and went through puberty when autism was merely whispered about, and it was neither understood nor of interest to the public at large.

If I were to have a detailed map which clearly laid out the landmarks of what roads to avoid during my trip, metaphorically speaking, I would have avoided such life events as changing residences and schools, living in different communities, moving to a foreign country and of course, facing a strange and unknown country and its people. But no such road map existed, certainly not for parents of AS adult children Yes, the book stores are flooded with advice books on good parenting practices, but when our son was growing up until the age of 12 in America , we were totally unaware of his diagnosis and condition.

Had we known that our son did indeed have an autistic spectrum disorder, we certainly would not have relocated so often, nor would we have immigrated to another country. Now, when his early adult years are filled with happy work days, outings with colleagues and good stories about encounters with strangers on the street or neighbors, I feel blessed, proud, and at ease with our life's choices. But on those awful days, when as an AS adult our son expresses anger and frustration over something which to us seems so uncomplicated and straightforward, I ask myself if moving him to a foreign environment as an adolescent was fair. Of course, none of these scenarios or soul-searching moments provides special insights about the rights and wrongs of child-rearing.

Dr. Peter Vermeulen, an autistic consultant and lecturer at the Autisme Centraal in Belguim, explores why the focus should be on raising the level of happiness in persons with ASD. He notes that the pursuit and attainment of emotional wellbeing is of great value for most people, but little attention is given to this subject among those with ASD. He emphasizes this by sharing his dismay that studies of the outcome of interventions seldom include the emotional satisfaction of the subject. When examining the autistic, objective criteria such as number of friends, cognitive and adaptive levels of functioning, and supports are addressed but their happiness is never considered. A good balance between protection and challenge should be a reasonable aim. What makes our autistic child flourish and the development of strategies to nurture his emotional wellbeing is our greatest challenge. Providing helpful interventions and education are important, but no less significant is being proud of what our children are able to do and giving them the opportunities to thrive. While our son was going through those trying teenage years, we yearned to find a way to give his life more stability and contentment. Our empathic psychologist, who worked tirelessly with our son, seemed to provide some of the tools he desperately sought and needed to become a happier teenager. By doing so, he helped prepare him emotionally to move forward into his college years.

Those adolescent years, even under the best circumstances, are trying and difficult for any child. Flooded with hormones that bring dramatic physical and emotional changes, intense mood swings, and coping with personal crises, the typical teenager sways through those years frantically trying to forge an identity which is authentically his own. Our AS adolescent children have an added component as their strange behaviors cannot be explained away as typically teenager antics. Being accepted as a member of the group and embraced by the opposite sex are rites of passage most teenagers manage to get through, but for our AS children, those expectations are simply unattainable. They lack the social insight to become one of the group and the understanding to interact appropriately with the opposite sex. Their often clumsy attempts to be a good team player are met with ridicule, distrust and sometimes even hostility. Efforts at reaching out to a girl can be inappropriate, bordering on what may be interpreted as overly aggressive sexual advances. These are turbulent times, characterized by extended periods of turmoil, upset and uncertainty. And for our family, those years can only be described as deeply painful and miserable.

Depression, anxiety and anger were emotions our son strongly demonstrated during his teenage years. The expression of his anger was often outbursts at his siblings and at us, his parents. His behavior was so unpredictable and inappropriate to a given situation, that we avoided entertaining and even inviting friends in for a cup of coffee. We never knew what might trigger an outburst. While he was never violent, he was a strapping young man with the physical potential to do harm. Still, I can't remember ever being fearful that his anger would spiral into hostile acts toward his family.

I do recall, however, that during the three years our elder son was serving in the Israel Defense Forces, we advised him not to bring home any weapons or ammunition. On the few very rare occasions when he was tasked by his unit to do so, we were sure to keep his gun carefully out of sight. This was truly heartbreaking for us. While we did not feel any imminent threat from our AS son, we were also keenly aware that we really did not understand what drove his extreme agitation, anger and anxiety. Attwood points out that an AS teenager can show signs of "externalized agitated depression" or blaming others rather than oneself as a response to the sense of alienation and marginalization so strongly perceived. Our son was painfully aware of being different and of being treated with the callousness that teenagers can dole out. This unfortunate situation, amongst others, would trigger the upsetting outbursts we experienced with our son. At one point when he was standing below one of the windows in our apartment, throwing mud and stones and shouting at us, our kind, soft-spoken elderly neighbors appeared at our door asking if there was anything they might do to help the family. While their concern was touching, it was also terribly embarrassing for us.

Our son was the middle child. I have no idea how his two siblings possessed such maturity and insight to grasp that our family was in distress but they were thoughtful of one another, always patient and comforting. It began to feel that we were undergoing role reversals in our family as our two kids became compassionate caretakers to their own parents. We shall always be grateful and appreciative of their compassion, empathy, and love during those turbulent years. It was as if our family unit was disintegrating before our very eyes, and my husband and I had no clue as to how to reverse the process. We lacked the guidance, control, and understanding to do whatever needed to be done to bring our son into the family with acceptance, unconditional love and patience. We were drained and lacked the will and clarity to safeguard our family and protect our other two children who seemed to remain incredibly calm and tolerant amidst the family chaos and turmoil. They often were our best source of support, a Rock of Gibraltar for us amidst a stormy sea of emotional exhaustion.

Craig Kendall, the author of many books on the subject of raising children on the spectrum, describes how "social innuendo" goes completely over the head of those with AS. He goes on to note that when the child becomes an adolescent at age 12 or 13, his simple world of talking about airplanes or rocks with a friend becomes unfamiliar as this companion begins to develop interests in dating, clothes and fashion, and social chats which are so foreign to the AS adolescent. He sagely advises parents to pay attention to the reality that their AS child has no interest or idea about how to dress, how to use social slang, how to behave in order to "fit in" to the world of the teenager. Doing this, he declares, does not come naturally. Social needs throughout the teenage years are important to consider; wise counsel written in 2009, and relevant today.

A recent short film clip that I watched called "Keep the Change" sensitively portrays how two young AS adults struggle to interact and find a common language of communication and understanding. This film represented to me the ongoing and persistent challenges faced by Asperger adolescents. Forging meaningful relationships, engaging in rather simple, uncomplicated every day activities, such as taking public transportation or shopping in both general and specialty shops, overwhelmed the young protagonist and brought him close to tears. To alleviate his sense of helplessness, the kindness and compassion shown by his female companion helped him to overcome his frustration. What was particularly moving were her genuine efforts to comfort him through her soothing touch and gaze, rather than attempting to modify his behavior. As I viewed this film, it was not clear to me whether or not she was capable of deciphering the social codes of conduct herself. What was certain, however, was that this display of affection, empathy and acceptance on her part helped him to push aside his sense of hurt caused by being scorned by the salesperson, or the bus and taxi drivers. At each encounter he handed the service person a twenty dollar bill, remarking to each one that they could "keep the change" obviously an expression he had picked up, rehearsed, overused and misused and a rather catchy title for the short film. In other words, someone somewhere had trained him to use this expression, but he was utterly incapable of judging the right circumstances for a stranger to, indeed, keep the change.

Our son's integration into his new community and school required that he not only master the language, but also understand nonverbal social cues and cultural nuances, difficult under the best of circumstances, but overwhelming to a child with an autistic syndrome diagnosis. Years of meltdowns in our backyard, constant shouting and fits of anger, irritable reactions and unruly behavior demanded our full time attention. After many searches, we were introduced to a kind, well-educated and Harvard trained psychologist who managed to earn the trust and respect of our son. Through weekly sessions that sometimes lasted hours, and over a period of several years, our son managed to navigate through those turbulent adolescent waters.

Gas Masks and High Grades

We took him out of the neighborhood school which I described previously and placed him in a more familiar environment, first in a boarding school for overseas students, mainly from the US and then to an American School about two hours from where we were living. During his years in the boarding school, we experienced the Gulf War and of course, living in Israel, were the target of ongoing missile attacks. In addition to adjusting to his new school settings, he was required to learn how to don a gas mask when the sirens screamed, how to find the closest shelter for protection from a missile attack, and how to survive in the sweltering heat of stuffy safe rooms equipped with emergency survival supplies. Most schools remained closed for several weeks during the war so he had the sense of being in a safe space provided by his family, both physically and emotionally. Perhaps it was this protection that gave him the security and self-confidence to do what was required during the awful nights filled with sirens going off, running for safety and enduring long hours in suffocating safe rooms. I remember speaking with my neighbor, a Canadian psychiatrist, about how his patients were coping. He was fascinated by how cooperative and willing they were to do what was necessary to get through those hours and days under attack. I described how well our son was coping under these circumstances and we both concluded that perhaps it was the survival instinct kicking in which helped them to function so well under such horrifying conditions.

And indeed, we did get through these times in the early 90s when nothing we had ever experienced before happened to us. Our lives were upended and the security and safety every parent seeks for their children became illusory. Once the Gulf War ended, though, it was rather amazing to see how quickly our lives returned to a normal, predictable rhythm and routine. Our son returned to his American School program where he was successful academically but, sadly, had no friends, no invitations to parties and no social life. He took a public bus early in the morning to arrive on time for his classes and occasionally stayed overnight with our friends who lived closer to his school. He had special support with his academic subjects and seemed to relish writing book reports and doing projects for which he always received high grades. His teachers reported that he was smart, cooperative and eager to learn. Neither they nor we considered his lack of social support to be detrimental to his academic achievements. The tantrums had pretty much run their course and he was relaxed and easy to be around at home. The illusion that everything was okay and that he would transfer from high school to college with the ease and self-assurance of his contemporaries was short-lived.

When the time came to choose between either getting drafted into the Israeli army or continuing his studies abroad, my son's options were limited by resources, the laws of the state requiring all young people at the age of 18 to register for compulsory military service, and geographical distance from family support. In the end, he decided to return to the US to attend Curry College in Milton, Massachusetts which seemed to have a very good reputation based on their experiences working with students with special needs.

Pain Perception and Piaget

An article in the *Spectrum News* by Sarah Deweerdt describes a recent, though unpublished, study conducted to determine how the brain in neurotypical adults differs from those identified with autism as related to pain experiences. Though the pool was small and I believe as such, it would be rather difficult to generalize the findings to an existing population, the conclusions are interesting and may shed some light on how the two populations experience, define and recover from pain. The images of brain activity of the pool of 17 autistic adults were compared with 16 neurotypicals when exposed to an unpleasant experience. How the perception of the experience of pain differed was interesting. The conclusions of the research suggested that for a short period of time after the painful stimulus, the images demonstrated that the brain in the control group was still responding, but among the autistic population, it no longer did. Once the pain had ceased, the brain image of the autistic population returned to what it had been before as though nothing had taken place. Initially it was found, the pattern of pain processing among the autistic group was similar to the control group, but the cognitive and emotional evaluation of pain varied among the two populations. In describing the experience, both groups reported similar pain thresholds however, even though both groups rated the level of pain exactly the same, their brains responded very differently. The neurotypical was still responding for as long as ten seconds later as though to say, "Hey, you were just in pain!" but the brain pattern of the autistic did not show a lingering effect. Once the experience was finished, it was as though nothing had happened just a brief moment earlier.

How much like my son's expressions of certain cognitive and emotional experiences. Once something was finished, it was as though it had never happened to him. His years in high school draw little interest or engagement in discussions I have tried to initiate. In a similar vein, his years living abroad, his studies at college or his experiences with a former girlfriend are events which seemed to have been safely and securely tucked away in the dark recesses of his memory. If I did not know his history myself, I would infer that these events, like the pain experience described above, never happened. Was it the associated or imagined trauma of these personal events which demanded that the event itself be suppressed or was it a thoughtful and managed self-imposed amnesia? I cannot pretend to know, but must admit, that at times it is upsetting, as if exposure and maturation are concepts only, and have little to do with the process of growing into adulthood.

As an educator and researcher myself, I hold a Ph.D. in English Language and Literature in addition to a formal teaching license. Thus, I have always been intrigued by the theories of the classic Swiss psychologist and educator, Jean

Piaget. As a university undergraduate and graduate student, I was intrigued by what he described as how we as children and later, adults, "come to know." Piaget's famous observation that children were not less intelligent than adults but rather think differently about their world is a critical starting point for attempting to understand the different ways of thinking between the neurotypical and the autistic. One is not less valid than the other, just different.

Piaget's influence as a developmental psychologist trained in biology and philosophy has had a far reaching impact in the fields of education and child development. To Piaget, cognitive development was a reorganization of mental processes as a result of experience and maturation, and the interactions between them. He posits that children construct an understanding of the environment and their immediate world, experience disconnects in what they know and discover through these experiences, all the while adjusting their notions and ideas accordingly. This ongoing process of exposure through experience and adjustment or development of new ways to assimilate this into something different is what constitutes knowledge and contributes to cognitive development.

As a result of Piaget's theories about the nature of knowledge and cognitive development, parents, teachers, caregivers and anyone working with young children are encouraged to provide a rich, challenging, and supportive environment, increasing the natural propensity to learn and grow.

Having studied Piaget both as a young student and in later years, as a mother interested in child development, how excited and pleased I was when our consulting psychiatrist recently said something very encouraging. He commented that our son's life appeared to be enriched by his experiences, challenged with work and independent living responsibilities and supported by staff and family members with whom he is in daily contact. It was a wonderful and rare moment of thinking that maybe, just maybe, his life will continue on a path of well-deserved rewards, fulfillment and happiness as only he could feel in his very special way. It was a moment when I took a step back to appreciate just how far he had come in his journey toward adulthood and a full life filled with promise and hope.

Returning to Piaget, I have to say that so many of his theories about cognitive development might be generalized to include the manner in which the AS population may learn to interact with the world, by acquiring knowledge through a complex and ongoing process of experiencing, sifting, reorganizing, and developing what Piaget refers to as *schema*. Assimilating this knowledge either into existing *schema* or groupings or creating an entirely new category of information by a process of accommodation or creating new categories of understanding the world, is, according to Piaget, the essence of intellectual development.

Most Asperger syndrome adults have had a variety of experiences in their world, some of which may have been ugly and frightening, but others hold promise for security and satisfaction. It is critical to their emotional well-being and cognitive development to provide a fertile field of exposure and rich opportunities for experience, precisely to allow this process of sifting, accommodation and assimilation to take place. New *schema* must be developed in order for them to be able to navigate the sometimes troubling waters of everyday living. It is my opinion and *raison d'être* for having him return to Israel to be close to his family that ongoing growth and development is not only a possibility, but an essential component of his overall well-being if he continues this process of experience, exposure, accommodation and assimilation. Regarding young children, Piaget's theories on acquiring knowledge about the complex world in which we live can be also applied to the young adult with Asperger syndrome. So much of our lives as parents of adults with this syndrome is spent trying to problem solve, understand and accept the ways of our children that we can easily overlook a fundamental and critical component in their development, exposing them to rich experiences in the form of perhaps travel, work challenges, and teaching them different ways of doing familiar tasks.

Misunderstood and Wrongfully Accused

How truly sad, therefore, to see how strange behaviors which are sometimes displayed among the autistic and, in particular, the Asperger population, can be generalized to describe brutal murderers acting out their psychopathy. Psychopathic behaviors as we understand them are not a part of the emotional makeup of Asperger adults. To jump to the conclusion that psychopathic behavior is a predictable outcome of those diagnosed on the spectrum is patently wrong and vicious.

To point out the cruel discrimination which some individuals with this disorder face, I would like to refer to an insightful and well-researched article in the *International New York Times* (2015). The author, Andrew Solomon, addresses the issue of AS diagnosis as it was linked to shootings on the college campus in Oregon, where Christopher Harper-Mercer killed and injured innocent bystanders, as well as the Newtown school and Columbine shootings. Harper-Mercer's mother claimed that both she and her son had Asperger syndrome. Shortly after this information made the round of news media, a Facebook page called "Families against Autistic Shooters" ranted about what they described as the dead eyes of the autistic, and stereotyped those on the spectrum as being cold and calculating killing machines, with no regard for human life. Lacking empathy, the rant continued, the recent snipers were obviously capable of such heinous crimes since they lacked human feelings, a deficit which they claimed was associated with autism. And this rant on a Facebook page continues using the social media technology of today, decades after Temple Grandin's mother completed her documentary. The film she created was an attempt to expose the serious lack of interest and concern for those poor souls who were committed to institutions and exiled from their families and communities, those autistic children born a generation too soon, one would hope.

Solomon makes a courageous, though undeserved effort, to understand how supposedly reasonable adults in the twenty-first century could continue to ascribe monstrous behavior to a group of individuals more often abused than abusers themselves. He suggests that such misunderstandings may arise due to confusions about the condition which manifests itself in a variety of symptoms and actions making any generalizations faulty. He notes, for example, that social awkwardness can be misunderstood as a lack of caring or empathy about another person. The personality of the autistic, he continues, fits the mosaic of any other individual. Some are kind and thoughtful, while others appear uncaring and distant. Some exhibit social anxiety while others show joy and happiness in a safe, friendly and accepting environment. Whatever characteristics we find among those diagnosed with AS, brutality is not generally associated with this group. Unfortunately, Andrew Solomon continues, profiling autistics as psychopaths is an insidious effort to stereotype, and one which leads to outrageous and dangerous claims about this vulnerable and weak population. Solomon's article is an outstanding narrative debunking the myth of the autistic as potential murderers.

The Road Taken Back

A few weeks before his 18th birthday, we packed our son up and took him to the airport for his flight back to the US and the start of a new chapter in his life. Aided with the remarkable support and generosity of family and friends, we were able to arrange his transition back to his familiar environment, culture and language. We were filled with hope that this return to his home that he had left seven years earlier would build his self-confidence and self-esteem and provide a springboard for a college life of a normative young adult. Unaware that he was suffering from the autism spectrum diagnosis, we had high hopes that our son would once again be a seemingly happy and well-rounded young man carving out his place in his world. While his psychologist worked hard to prepare him and his family for this transition, we believed that his unusual patterns of behavior would dissipate as he re-adjusted to his home country. Since we did not know that he had AS, these expectations were utterly unrealistic and completely off track. Working on the premise that a change in environment results in a change in behavior, we were totally unprepared for what was ahead. We thought that his high school years had been trying, while he was living at home under our care and supervision. Little did we understand how a young adult, living on his own and without family support or supervision could lose his way as he struggled with alienation, separation and anxiety.

Because our son was academically talented, he was able to finish his undergraduate program in three rather than the standard four years. However, his undergraduate degree in history and communication offered no credentials in helping him to secure employment. In addition, in a similar pattern to his high school years, his college experience did not include developing friendships or securing lifelong relationships. His college graduation ceremony which I attended was extraordinary. To this day, I have a photograph of him receiving his diploma on my desk. He was standing tall, a proud young man, so filled with the sense that his future would be brimming with promise and possibilities.

Although he was delighted with his new status as a college graduate and eager to join the work force, he was uncertain about which direction he might take.

During his college years, he was unable to live in the college dormitory as the other students were, according to his accounts, too noisy, rambunctious and drank too much. After a struggle, it was finally agreed that he would have his own room and in fact, to this day, he lives independently rather than in a group home. He spent his spare time studying and working in the library as a work study arrangement and did a short stint as a DJ for the college radio. He absolutely refused my requests to visit and over the next three years in college, while I wrote to him weekly and sent packages to him filled with his favorite snacks, he never once responded. It was as though he had shut himself off completely from his family living abroad. His father occasionally did visit with him, but his holidays were spent with family in the States and during vacation periods he attended summer school programs at his college and at the University of Massachusetts. He was very comfortable in this academic environment though he had virtually no friends and no social life of which we were aware. His books were his best pals, just as they were when he was a youngster growing up. We were hopeful that he would stay in school and go on to graduate studies, but the circumstances were such that this was not possible. So he was thrust into the world of work for which he had little preparation and awareness.

We applied our familiarity with a typical young adult to our son who, at that time, was still undiagnosed. Our other two children were serving in the army and attending university in Israel. They transitioned with ease from high school to army and then to the university. Our son, however, found the transition from the somewhat protective college environment to the adult workforce overwhelming and scary. We never considered that his good college record, friendliness and ability to express himself would not compensate for his lack of social skills and his inability to understand even basic social cues and fundamental requirements for living such as paying bills, driving, and maintaining a healthy and safe living environment.

Our family strategy was to encourage him to find his own way at his own pace and we would take a step back. Unfortunately, we did not understand that social connections and close family support were absolutely crucial for a young adult with AS. We assumed that he would not only embrace independence, but thrive on being self-sufficient, and responsible for his life in a way he found suitable and comfortable. Over the next several years, we watched in painful horror as his situation deteriorated.

Every religious holiday was celebrated by his coming back to Israel to visit with us. This actually meant that he flew to Israel two or three times annually and we went to the US to spend time with him several times a year. All told, we saw him approximately every other month as we were very soon acutely aware that even those friends who mentioned that they would be happy to invite him for a visit seemed to vanish. Family members expressed interest and concern but he was never invited for a home visit. I guess that the understanding was a child who can finish college can also establish residence, fit into a community and find suitable employment. We, his immediate family, knew better. Family and friends had shown extraordinary kindness toward him during his college years. He was invited to spend holidays with them, visit with them during school recess, and spend some summer months hanging out in their homes. This all changed when he moved to Atlanta to "be on his own". Expectations were so unrealistic but we really did hope and pray that he would find a good life in a supportive and accepting community known for its friendliness and outreach to newcomers. Our son, however, simply did not fit the profile and we soon understood that this decision to relocate him to an unfamiliar community would be something that we would seriously regret later on.

Chapter 6

Lost and Lonely in Atlanta

Heartbreak in a "Fun" City

Our son decided to remain in the US, and after getting some advice, we thought that moving him to Atlanta, Georgia was a good choice. At that time in the early 90s, Atlanta was known to be a popular destination for young people searching for work opportunities, social clubs, pleasant weather and a slower pace of living. The city was brimming with the energy and vitality that comes with a more youthful population. Restaurant, bars and discos were packed with young people who worked hard during the day and played hard in the evening hours. Newspapers, magazines, and public announcements offered what seemed to be unlimited opportunities for those in search of friendships and romance, along with social events and elective courses. Rental apartments were available at reasonable rates. Our impression was that this city had the perfect blend of work, fun, and a healthy environment. We were so pleased with our decision to relocate our son to the hospitable south that we did not consider the challenges such a move brought with it.

Once we settled him in a simple but well-located apartment, helped him search for a job and get acclimated to his new city, we returned home, 6,000 miles away. He was left pretty much to fend for himself. Our reasoning was since he had developed a good sense of how to cope with many challenges as an independent college student, he certainly was prepared to face the challenges any other young adult faced such as seeking out a social network, setting up job interviews, and taking care of his basic needs. He remained in contact with us and we spoke by telephone on a regular basis.

He did work in several low-paying, menial jobs in Atlanta, but was unable to sustain any of them long-term or find a position which might offer him opportunities for growth and development. His performance did not fit his potential nor did it square with his excellent college education. We watched as he struggled to maintain his dignity and self-respect as one boss after another mistreated, ignored or simply fired him following a brief stint of employment. We often wondered why he, in particular, was singled out for such shabby treatment. Little did we know back then that this uncaring attitude was more commonplace among persons in the community who were ignorant of the strange behaviors typical of autistic individuals. What we perceived as strange behaviors could be misinterpreted by an uninformed supervisor as threatening and menacing.

One of our son's proudest moments came when he was hired to work in security at the Atlantic Olympic Games in the summer of 1996. He also volunteered as a guide in a local historical museum, which meant also being trained, wearing proper dress and memorizing many details about the South during the Civil War. When we visited him at one point, we went along to the museum and watched as he made his historically accurate presentation to a small group of visitors. He was well-informed but seemed disconnected from his audience. His volunteering came to an abrupt halt one day for reasons which made little sense, when he was told to leave. How does a volunteer get fired? We were saddened to learn about his dismissal but helped him to reframe this experience so he could move forward.

While living in a rather large apartment complex, he met a neighbor who became his partner and girlfriend. She counseled him, encouraged him to find suitable work and was his best friend. Predictably, however, the relationship collapsed as he was unable to meet either her social or emotional needs. She was a sweet and caring young lady but was not aware of the needs of a man on the spectrum, and how could she be? He was saddened when she decided to move back to her home town in the Midwest and they severed all contact. To this day, he still mentions her name when referring to past girlfriends, and speaks fondly of the times they spent together. He does not, however, feel any sense of responsibility for the failed relationship nor does he appear interested in understanding how such a relationship had developed, flourished and then crumbled apart.

Oliver Sacks: Celibacy and a Neurology of Identity

Ever since this relationship with his friend and neighbor ended, he has chosen celibacy over intimacy, a position he defends as part of his understanding of Jewish law and tradition. It is a reasonable, logical decision, very personal and private, and one which we fully understand and respect. As Dr. Oliver Sacks, the famous neurologist who died recently noted in one of his interviews, he chose celibacy later in life as a response to his self-awareness that intimacy presented interpersonal obligations he was unable and unwilling to fulfill and take upon himself. Recently reading some of Sacks' writings about his journey as a medical doctor with a special interest in mentally disadvantaged persons, I am struck by his sensitivity and descriptions of his patients many of whom other doctors had given up on. We are more familiar with some of his work as portrayed through the heartwarming performances by Robin Williams and Robert de Niro in the Hollywood movie "Awakenings" but on a deeper, more philosophical level, the work which Sacks has done over many years has brought with it a certain level of awareness of vulnerable persons with a multitude of neurological impairments including Tourettes syndrome and AS. One of his most oft-quoted lines reflects his incredible empathy for his patients when he comments that he is also an honorary Asperger, suspecting that "we all have a bit of everything."

In a *New York Times* article entitled "A Brain with a Heart" (2012) Sacks is being interviewed, and he speaks about a neurology of identity, noting that affected patients often build an identity in part through their battles with their own dysfunctional selves. To a certain degree, he elaborates, we are all flawed but we try to find ways consistent with humanity to live, not by pill-popping but by coming to terms with our own condition.

The Scientific Genius of Henry Cavendish

Regarding the scientist Henry Cavendish and the speculation that he may have suffered from Asperger syndrome, Dr. Fred Volkmar has noted, unfortunately, a sort of "cottage industry" has emerged suggesting that most people have a touch of Asperger. This is a comment I hear from people who try to show their understanding of this condition by pointing to some of their own eccentricities. I find these observations annoying and insulting but, on the other hand, I suppose that this is an attempt to show empathy and awareness of this condition. Far from contradicting Oliver Sack's wry comment about all of us having flaws, the notion that AS is present in most people, but is expressed in a variety of ways, seems to me to be an oversimplification of those on the spectrum.

In Henry Cavendish's biography (2015), Steve Silberman makes a point of stressing that while the scientist himself was perceived as idiosyncratic, his work was devoted to his single-minded passion which was to increase the sum of human knowledge. Silberman states that in his valiant and fascinating efforts to reach his all-consuming goal, he was described by colleagues at Cambridge and other acquaintances as arrogant, selfish, snobbish, disdainful of others, cold and indifferent. Charles Blagden, one of the few scientists welcomed into Cavendish's personal life as the latter become the mentor to the young scientist, mentions that Cavendish, while appearing to be a man of little affection, in fact, actually meant well.

Silberman relates how one of the most telling accounts of Cavendish's scientific accomplishments and personality were written by the well-known chemist at the time, George Wilson. In describing Cavendish both as a scientist and a human being, Wilson observed that his emotional life was comprised of "negations" including a lack of ability to love, hate, fear, or hope. These strange traits and emotional voids, according to the biographer Wilson, allowed the scientist the mental framework and ability to focus in a manner which transcended human foibles, frailties and needs.

While this is certainly an interesting characterization of Cavendish, it remains speculative, indeed, if he could have suffered from an autism spectrum disorder. Evidence, according to Silberman, certainly points in this direction but, it seems like a rather giant leap to assume that a genius as well established as Cavendish did indeed have such a diagnosis. As a recluse whose view of the universe came from a very different perspective, Cavendish's inherited wealth gave him every opportunity afforded to a mortal to pursue his interest and life's work without having to be bothered with the everyday issues that preoccupy the average person.

Dr. Volkmar notes that many AS sufferers tend to engage in what he describes as "an endless acquisition of facts" which does not predispose them to anything considered productive by the standard of Western culture. In contrast, Cavendish, as noted, gained scientific information which he then applied to his quest for knowledge. The process of acquisition of knowledge and its application to the human condition, in a sense, may disqualify Cavendish as having an AS diagnosis. Cavendish, unlike those whom Volkmar describes, appears to have had a keen understanding of humanity and his desire to contribute indicates a very strong connection to it. Volkmar observes that this AS tendency of acquiring facts for its own sake may in fact interfere with any degree of real accomplishment.

Our son, for example, can lecture on complex topics for which he has a keen interest, often seemingly oblivious to not only those around him, but also to the relevance of what he has to say. This strange behavioral pattern, also described by Volkmar, may be aptly applied to those with AS who, as Henry David Thoreau claimed "lead lives of quiet desperation." Therefore, they are continually challenged by a deep and personal sense of social estrangement and marginalization. It seems somewhat unfair, however, to assume that most spectrum disorder adults are doomed to lead lives of alienation and meaninglessness, caught up in a wave of self-stimulation and lack of human connections. Different, yes, but not necessarily less.

Temple Grandin: An Exemplary Woman

Even the most successful and well-known individuals on the spectrum are not exempt from similar social stigmatization and failures at work as my son has experienced and with which he continues to suffer. Temple Grandin stands out as an example of an accomplished scientist as do others diagnosed with this condition. The very fact that Dr. Grandin, who today is nearly 70 years old, continues to receive so much publicity is due to the exceptionality of who she is, especially as described by her mother, Eustacia Cutler, in her moving book published in 2004, *A Thorn in My Pocket*.

Cutler details the family struggle as Temple's father attempts to institutionalize her at an early age primarily due to a basic lack of understanding and acceptance of his little girl with autism. The book is fascinating to read as it describes the arduous, painful road the mother takes in her search for answers and appropriate responses to her daughter's strange behaviors. Money, obviously, was not an issue as she was given private tutorials, the best psychiatric supervision, outstanding private day schools, and the freedom to explore alternative life styles for herself as well as her family. When she took upon herself the quest to conduct research for a documentary on juvenile psychiatric hospitals in her New England community, Temple's mother journeyed to a variety of settings, such as penal institutions and detention centers where undiagnosed autistics often can be found.

Cutler described one place in which the children appeared to be not only isolated, sedated and silent, but in a trance, obsessed with repetitive and irrelevant preoccupations. One well-meaning physician even implored her not to write about these "stubborn children" as he described the patients, since the doctors really did not know how to treat them. Autism at the time of Cutler's research in the 50s was considered to be a disorder with psychosocial roots. Another doctor whom she interviewed acknowledged that he had a child with autism. His sage advice to Temple's mother was to "improvise and figure it out as you go along!"

Ignored and Invisible as Adults

We, the parents and family who count among us our children, siblings, spouses and other close relatives with AS, struggle with some basic notions about the meaning and quality of life of our adult loved ones. It is an existential soliloquy we carry on in our minds as we go through the motions of the mundane tasks of our lives. Having a framework, however, in terms of deep-seated religious beliefs and moral values can certainly help us to meet the challenges demanding our almost daily attention.

We worry when we read that depression is not uncommon among adult men with autism and that other psychiatric disorders such as ADHD, anxiety and obsessive-compulsive disorder can accompany those with an autism diagnosis.

In fact, Christopher Gillberg, professor of child and adolescent psychiatry at the University of Gothenburg in Sweden reminds us that anyone working with the AS population needs to be keenly aware of these problems. Tinca Polderman, assistant professor of complex genetics at the University of Amsterdam in the Netherlands, talks about the comorbidity of such mental conditions, and of a "blurred boundary" of different disorders. She hypothesizes that this overlap stems perhaps from some "biological glitch", as the various categories used to describe some psychiatric conditions including autism and AS overlook certain biological factors that are not strictly limited to each disorder. In other words, the categories established to describe and define one condition may in fact spill over and be appropriately applied to other existing biological conditions.

As parents of adults diagnosed on the spectrum, we worry when we read accounts such as those so poignantly described by Eli Gottlieb in his *New York Times* piece, "Adult, Autistic and Ignored" In 2015, Gottlieb wrote about his fifty plus older brother who was institutionalized at a young age in what appeared to be a pleasant residential facility. Following his mother's death in 2010, he became the custodian of his older sibling, and was stunned by how unchartered the waters were in what he describes as the "island nation of adult autism". In his introspective and extremely well-documented piece, Gottlieb discusses what he calls the "vast autism infrastructure" development. In his opinion, this is a response to the supposed rising incidence of children diagnosed on the spectrum, one in 68, a number which I have continued to use as a current yardstick for the diagnosis of child autism in the US.

Gottlieb notes that a vast array of services have sprung up as an effort to respond to the increase in numbers among the younger population, somewhat of a "big tent" approach. He also declares that these services include new schools, activist and advocacy organizations, social media, websites, and legislation guaranteeing civil and educational rights of those with disabilities. But, he comments with a sense of urgency and irony, these children eventually do grow into adulthood.

To further support Gottlieb's claim, recent statistics in the US suggest that approximately 500,000 children diagnosed on the autism spectrum will be 21 years of age or older in the next decade. As adults on the spectrum, nearly 90%

are either unemployed or underemployed. As young adults who completed high school, nearly 40% are thus ineligible for services. State funding, Gottlieb finds, seems to be based on some magical notion that this early adulthood autistic population will rather smoothly transition into employable, functional adults without any special support or guidance.

Indeed, he comments, this type of thinking forms a "larger disconnect" as currently, there is little to no national conversation about the fate of the autistic middle-aged or elderly person. Gottlieb contends that the limited money that has been earmarked for support or research might be put to better use assisting those currently residing in the homes of their aged parents, or residential communities, or even in mental institutions. In addition, he points out, very little is known about health issues linked to their long-term care or about how their condition may impact on maturational changes. He quotes Dr. Joseph Piven, professor of psychiatry, pediatrics and psychology at the University of North Carolina, that there is "virtually no knowledge base" about adults with autism.

In terms of cost analysis, Gottlieb believes that it is not sufficient to simply "throw money at adult autism"; instead, what he recommends is to begin a real deployment of services and a "seat at the table" of discussions surrounding policies at both the state and federal levels. He quotes a person working within the community where his brother currently resides as a call for financial expenditures for lifelong learning opportunities as well as longitudinal studies on the needs of the adult population. This suggestion has been echoed by both Dr. Piven and Louis Reichardt, director of the Simmons Foundation Autism Research Initiative.

Calling for better diagnostic tools in an aged autistic population, Deborah Rudacille notes that the Asperger syndrome diagnosis often emerges only after a major disruption in their lives fuels high anxiety and depression. In an article by Rudacille fittingly entitled "Invisible People" (2011), the author claims that for the elderly population, autism is almost an invisible condition, sometimes misdiagnosed, rarely treated and generally ignored. In a study entitled "Diagnosing Autism Spectrum Disorders in Elderly People" published in 2011 in the *International Psychogeriatrics Journal*, it is acknowledged that seniors with AS received their diagnosis many years later in their lives. They were described by family members as emotionally remote, rigid, inflexible and socially awkward. The team of authors also point out that it took decades for the Asperger syndrome to come to the attention of the English-speaking world. Fourteen years after the diagnosis of autism appeared in the Diagnostic and Statistical Manual of Mental Disorders in 1994, Asperger syndrome was included, only to be folded into the autism spectrum disorder over the following decades, as pointed out earlier, in the DSM 5 revision.

Both these articles lament the fact that diagnosis often comes too late in the lives of these invisible people. The latter article describes three men, aged 72, 78, and 83 at the time of publication, all of whom were married and were fathers. After becoming a widower, one was admitted to a psychiatric unit, and the second man was admitted to a residential psychiatric unit. The last man was sent to a facility after their son was diagnosed with PDD and the man's wife connected this diagnosis to her husband's behaviors. Certainly not a pretty picture of what the future may hold for the currently aging and diagnosed population. These factors—late diagnosis, and being ignored and neglected by society—are sufficient for my angst about my son and his uncertain future.

Looking Ahead: Parental Duties

Not giving in to pessimism or hopelessness, however, I would like to support the contention that early diagnosis, ongoing, consistent and professional interventions, and good support systems—including proper supervision of the caregivers, and family acceptance and understanding—all go a long way to ensure that this population not end up like those three men described in the journal. Indeed the path of our elders, who should be respected, revered and treasured as honorable members of our community, is to psychiatric facilities, not an outcome to be proud of in the twenty-first century. I strongly feel that as a mother of one diagnosed with AS, it is my obligation to oversee my child's care and prepare carefully for his future. It is my duty to do this in order to prevent such an unfortunate outcome, of a life perhaps well-lived but not carefully managed, so as to avoid psychiatric institutionalization as an elderly person.

As my parental responsibilities include the cost of supporting my son's wellbeing and continued maintenance, I feel obliged to also consider the cost to not only the family, but society as a whole. It is estimated that in one year alone, autism will cost the US about 1.5% of the GDP, a figure which could balloon from $268 billion in 2015 to $461 billion in a decade. To put these figures into some type of perspective, the "cost of autism" in 2015 is on par with the estimated cost of diabetes, and more than 5 times the cost of expenses related to stroke or hypertension. David Mandell, as quoted earlier, found that the lifetime cost of one autistic individual is $1.4 million and increases by another million dollars for an autistic person with an intellectual disability. Researchers take a somewhat more optimistic approach when they describe the increase in current expenditures for behavioral interventions as halving the costs of the young adult populations.

Dealing with the current costs of looking after the needs of the adult population, Mandell points out, suggests a business as usual approach. He contends that if society does not get better at helping those adults with autism and delivering efficient care while keeping them in their communities, then the economic toll will tally up beyond expected calculations. Furthermore, as noted above, their lives are doomed to likely end with costly institutionalization.

Given the current state of treatments, care, and supervision of adults on the spectrum, it should not come as a surprise to see an increased rate of diagnosis of additional mental disorders amongst those on the spectrum, including anxiety disorders. Our son, for example, was recently found to have high blood pressure, a medical condition usually associated with elevated anxiety levels. How to predict, plan for, and deal with what may in fact be a significant increase in the rate of other psychiatric disorders is a challenge not only for the families but for services designed to meet the needs of those on the spectrum including, medical and housing services.

Islands of Solitude

Anxiety issues often associated with a spectrum diagnosis are today recognized and addressed by many writers in the field of autism studies. "Islands of solitude" is an expression Tony Attwood uses when describing the intense and often debilitating anxiety experienced by those with AS who must have a place to turn to so this social anxiety can be blunted. As a speaker at the Third Annual Day of Learning sponsored by the Autism Science Foundation, April, 2016, Dr. Alex

Kolevzon noted that approximately 40% of those on the spectrum have formal anxiety disorders, and 30% also suffer from phobias, such as fear of medications. Being on the spectrum can be viewed as both a cause and consequence of anxiety, Dr. Kolevzon explains. Effective social skills and communication activities can be severely impaired as a result of the anxiety disorder. Fear of losing control may be treated with a pharmacological approach or nonmedical intervention. Using medications, he maintains, has some limited evidence supporting this method. Applying adaptation skills using visual supports, repetition and practice can be very effective in reducing the severity of anxiety seen among this population. As we understand it and as applied to the AS population, this anxiety can be described as an inappropriate, exaggerated response to a given situation, a loss of control using Kolevzon's description, and consequently a distorted interpretation of what is actually happening. Clinically, I like to think of it as an expression or extension of a learning disability, in a sense, an LD of thinking, a distortion of a perceived threat.

There are ways of minimizing this LD of the mind, as I call it, for example, by giving the young adult a secure and safe place to go when social anxiety becomes too intense. Children, for example, can be encouraged to go on an errand which gives them some time for solitude. Alternatives to full school days can benefit these children who are not able to cope with a full school schedule. An adult might find solitude in doing crossword puzzles, listening to classical music or a good relaxation ritual such as Yoga. Our son, for example, enjoys listening to classical music and relaxing in a neighborhood gym. It has also been suggested that using a computer as a distracter can help override the intense feelings of anxiety which can accompany social interactions, especially when working with adults on the spectrum.

Attwood has observed that prolonged periods of severe anxiety can lead to a psychiatric secondary condition such as obsessive compulsive disorder (OCD). Hoarding, over attention to cleanliness and other expressions of OCD behaviors may operate as a means to reduce anxiety. Our son, for example, before moving into an apartment closer to his place of work began to hoard items such as shoes, shirts and jeans to the extent that when he actually moved in to his new home, there were so many bags filled with these items, that there was hardly room to move about. After intensive attention and careful work with a coach, he was able to let go of much of what he had accumulated by agreeing to box the items, carefully labeling the contents and receiving permission from the other tenants to place the bins, over 75 of them, in a designated storage area. However, the classical diagnosis of hoarding is not applicable to people on the autism spectrum disorder for they have different triggers for this behavior.

Cognitive Behavior Therapy or CBT as it is popularly known, as an approach to the way the AS person thinks about and reacts to anxiety might be used by a clinical psychologist to treat severe anxiety. While our son does work with a therapist, CBT is not an effective approach in helping him to deal with his frequent bouts of high anxiety. Temple Grandin describes how her severe anxiety and associated depression were significantly reduced by the range of medications referred to as Selective Serotonin Reuptake Inhibitors or the class of drugs known as SSRIs. These pills, she claims, have changed her life. Of course there is a rigorous and robust debate about the appropriateness and use of SSRI medications among the AS population and clearly, its use is a very personal and private decision between the AS patient and his or her psychiatrist. Our consulting psychiatrist, for example, felt that in our son's case, the use of SSRIs was counter-indicated and did not advise prescribing these psychiatric medications, a position we are comfortable supporting.

Odd Jobs: From Hardware Store to Funeral Parlor

Finding and holding on to appropriate employment, in my opinion, is the most important and challenging task a young AS adult must face. The literature addressing employment among this population is often dismal and pessimistic, filled with sad stories of rejection, anxiety, and disappointments. As noted earlier, about 90% of those on the spectrum are either not employed or underemployed. In a research article entitled "Mapping the Needs of People with Asperger Syndrome" (2015), Yonatan Drori reports that the ability of the adult with AS to integrate into any work force is a challenge. A work mentor, he suggests, can help both the boss and the employee identify strengths such as intelligence and attention to detail so common in this population. When these strengths are both recognized and used appropriately, this can help to ease the adult into the workforce community. Our son's journey to meaningful and productive employment underscores the difficulties faced by an educated high functioning autistic young male adult.

My son worked in a call center, neighborhood hardware store and for a short-term stint, as a security guard at the Atlanta Olympics. These transitory jobs were followed by weeks and weeks of unemployment, resulting in days with nothing important or challenging to do with his time. He did try to join the local community center in order to swim and work out but this was also for brief and intermittent periods. Time was going by and he was seemingly not engaged in the community, social activities or work. He spent his days on the computer and roaming around in the neighborhood parks. In fact, the police once questioned him while he was loitering in a park and appeared to be looking strangely at people and even in some windows. To this day we do not know how accurate his descriptions were but we do know that this encounter with the authorities increased his fear of going out and even attempting to find meaningful outlets for his social needs. He became even more isolated and reclusive when his girlfriend, whom I described earlier, left the community.

We got him a secondhand car as public transportation was limited and he had learned how to drive several years earlier. While his car gave him mobility and we had hoped, opportunities to go out into the community, it actually became stressful as he struggled to figure things out such as how to change a tire and monitor the mechanical aspects of car ownership. What we had assumed would be a source of pleasure, convenience and comfort became an anxiety-producing burden. Later in his life when he returned to Israel, a heating or air conditioning system or even an oven provoked similar attacks of anxiety as he tried to master its usage. Dealing with mechanical or electronic devices, we came to understand, was simply overwhelming and until their usage was mastered, it had the potential to create untold episodes of extreme anxiety.

Interestingly, he learned how to operate a washer and dryer with minimal difficulties but was not able to apply this understanding to other household appliances and objects. Just recently he took along with him on a trip to Crete and Rhodes a fairly new camera and was so pleased with the numerous colorful photos he took of picturesque sites and other points of interest during his trip.

Many were taken of the same thing, but no doubt, the joy of capturing special moments far outweighed the repetitive scenes.

However, it took many months of coaxing and explaining before he agreed to even consider taking along this camera. We are now struggling with a similar issue of having him use a smartphone. On one hand, we feel that having access to this device could enhance his ability to communicate. On the other hand, we know from past experience that what we think of as a gift, or a useful device, can be perceived by him as just another layer of technology which can be a source of frustration and worry.

As part of our effort to guide him to find meaningful employment in Atlanta, a dear friend connected him to the local Jewish mortuary. Part of the ritual associated with traditional Jewish funerals is thoroughly washing the dead body and wrapping it in a shroud before putting it into the simple pine casket. Both embalming and viewing are prohibited by Jewish law. Preparations are highly ritualized and include the services of a *shomer* or guardian who remains with the body throughout the funeral and burial. Many communities, in fact, provide this service of a guardian to the body if a family member is unavailable. It is part of the tradition of showing respect to the deceased not to leave the body unattended and is considered a good deed of the highest order to watch over it. Psalms are recited by the *shomer* as he stands vigil over the deceased.

Our son was interviewed by the funeral director, who was impressed by his knowledge of Jewish tradition and customs. On the spot, the director hired him to be the *shomer* when a member of the Jewish community passed away. Our son was trained by the most experienced person in the community and accompanied him to learn more about the new role he had assumed. This middle-aged man was an observant member of the congregation, who showed great kindness and acceptance toward our son and some of his strange ways. Although they worked together for several years, our son was never invited to the man's family home for a visit, a meal or a holiday. There was clearly some sort of disconnect between work and family obligations, and therefore hosting a single, young adult male who had recently arrived to the community was not viewed as an obligation or a good deed. Socially, once again, our son was even more estranged, as watching over a dead body and reciting psalms was not exactly a recipe for social integration into the community. He was actually well paid, and often called upon to work in the funeral home. His generous uncle provided him with the appropriate dark suits and ties which he kept hanging neatly in his Atlanta apartment. Nonetheless, whenever we visited, we hauled all his soiled white shirts and suits to the dry cleaners.

For the first year in the funeral home, he seemed to be satisfied and pleased with his ability to earn a good living. However, he was very anxious about how to support himself and obtain permission to remain in his apartment. As an expression of his worries over how to sustain his living situation, he went to the front rental office and offered to give them a year's payment in advance if they could assure him that he would be welcome to stay. At this point, we found him a nice place to live attached to a local synagogue. The little house was separate from the synagogue, but because it was so close, he was able to participate in religious services and other events. We later learned that he often went to social gatherings uninvited and partook of the meals which had been prepared for the guests.

We were so saddened to hear that, even though he had his very own apartment right next door, he also went into the sanctuary itself and slept on the hard wooden pews when services were not being held. There were other strange behaviors which began to concern the leaders of the synagogue and we were asked to speak to our son to explain appropriate social behaviors. The leaders of this particular synagogue were kind and understanding, but obviously distressed by some of his ways which seemed so weird and inappropriate. His personal hygiene was lacking as was his judgment about conduct befitting one living on the premises. He was never menacing or aggressive, but simply strange to the people around him.

A Heartbreaking Downward Spiral

At one point we contacted the local welfare service to discuss ways in which they might integrate him into the community, including social events. When we met with them, how unprepared we were for the announcement that they actually knew our son well. He had registered with them as a homeless man! He thus had begun to think of himself as so alienated and unwelcome that he actually believed he had no home. We were distraught and overcome with pain and anguish. We quickly looked for ways to provide him with an anchor, one which would be challenging and suitable, and even consistent with his intellectual capacity. The funeral director suggested that he register for a year-long training course to become qualified as a funeral home employee. As he seemed to like his job as a *shomer*, we thought it was a good opportunity for him to learn, grow, and even develop some social connections. The school was quite a distance from where he had been living, but he took several dry runs to the school and eventually felt comfortable enough to go to the campus on his own. He seemed pleased and eager to be in a learning framework. The curriculum was challenging and he was up to the task of studying subjects necessary to become licensed. He enrolled in the program, attended classes and seemed content to once again be in an intellectually-stimulating environment. Nearly half a year passed and we were all relieved and pleased.

Then along came the inevitable snag. As part of his studies, he was required to participate in an embalming class. Citing traditional Jewish law which prohibited embalmment, he absolutely refused to attend the course, thereby canceling any possibility that he could graduate and move into a prosperous field. He was inflexible, unwilling to agree to some compromise, such as attending but not actually performing an embalmment. The school, of course, had strict regulations regarding the subject and would not agree to any further accommodations. The door was closed to him.

The next few years remain a blur in my memory. I recall going to his apartment to clean and disinfect it and finding an open can of dog food in his refrigerator. I remember seeing him sitting outside his little house, surrounded by weeds, wrecked cars and empty lots, all alone and looking so lost. I can still hear his sad and frightened voice on the telephone when he called to say he had "adopted" a homeless man who was begging on the street. According to his understanding of our tradition of being thoughtful and generous, our son had invited this stranger into his home for a meal and a shower. And a good deed it was. So good, in fact, that the homeless man absolutely refused to leave his home. We suggested giving him some cash and sending him on his way. He did this, but the poor fellow showed up again the following day. By this time, we were getting concerned as he had also been talked into giving him his only TV. We contacted the social welfare agency and got the police involved. It took several visits, but he finally agreed to cooperate with the authorities and to call them should the homeless man return. He never did, but the memory of those frantic late night calls and the sound of his voice quivering in fear still send chills up my spine.

Visits to his untidy home were unpleasant and upsetting. At this point, we engaged the help of another social service agency who sent over their social worker to meet him. The social worker took a personal interest in his welfare and tried, unsuccessfully, to engage him in activities sponsored by the center. Though initially suspicious and uncomfortable, he eventually did agree to go on some social outings and while he appeared to enjoy himself, he flatly refused to continue.

We had a weekly conversation with Paul, the outreach professional who made an earnest attempt to involve him in many activities, including accompanying groups on tours to museums both as a group member and a leader. After nearly a year, Paul suggested that we try to encourage him to return to Israel to be near family but reminded us that the decision would ultimately have to be his. I vividly remember the phone call when our son asked what we thought about his returning to Israel. We tried to remain calm and not overreact, not wanting him to hear how extremely pleased we were by his question. In our excitement, we booked flights for the following week and arranged to move his things up north to be put in storage with family to later be shipped back to Israel. His return was such a relief for us. He arrived back in Israel in January, 2001, three months after the outbreak of the Second Intifada and exactly 6 months before 9/11.

During the five year period of his stay in Atlanta, things had changed at home. We sought professional help to try to give a name to a condition which was so baffling and upsetting. After a long and arduous search, we decided upon a respected, Cambridge trained psychiatrist who was doing some good work with patients whose odd ways seemed to match our son's behavioral patterns. At our very first meeting, after a long and detailed description of his personal growth and development, the doctor asked us many questions about his behavior which at the moment, seemed a bit strange. During all those years of working so intensely with our son's psychologist, we had never been asked to relate to how he handled issues such as change and social situations, what were his fears and expectations, or if he had friendships which had been meaningful and sustainable throughout his high school and college years.

After a very long session, the psychiatrist suggested that we begin to read about a biological neurological disorder called Asperger syndrome and invited us to bring our son to meet him when he returned to Israel. In parting, he gave us some articles to take with us on the topic. It was a good thing he did, since I could neither remember nor spell this unfamiliar word Asperger. He did elaborate somewhat on the manifestations of AS and I do recall his mentioning that it was a syndrome on the autism spectrum, a total shock to both my husband and myself. But along with the initial shock came a sense of relief as well. Predictably, we searched for and read anything and everything we could find about Asperger Syndrome, mostly from books we shipped in from the States, as the subject was not yet part of the discourse here in Israel.

Coming Back to a Changed Home

During those Atlanta years, my husband's mother passed away and our son came to the funeral dressed for work. With unusual self-confidence, he accompanied the coffin and urged people to move along during the funeral procession. He seemed so pleased with his role as a *shomer*, that people commented about the deep respect he demonstrated for his beloved grandmother. But while other family members and grandchildren cried and grieved over the loss of a loved one, our son expressed no sadness. We, of course, rationalized that he was too preoccupied overseeing the funeral arrangements to connect emotionally to what was going on around him. He simply distanced himself from the situation, and while correct and friendly, his behavior seemed bizarre within the context of the death of a close family member.

This thirty-something young man, who was educated, well-traveled, and good looking, was so different from what we had experienced both with our other two children and from observing the development and life cycles of our friends' children. Our son's return to Israel at nearly age 30 was not at all what we had expected or planned for. Fortunately, we had been reading almost all the available autobiographies, nonfiction accounts of persons on the spectrum as well as a growing body of nonfiction books which suddenly caught the attention of a curious population. In addition, we searched for possible "solutions" to help cure our son or at least reduce his troubling symptoms. As Shannon Des Roches Rosa described so well in her recent article in the Autism Research News Spectrum, we also supplemented his diet with multiple alternative types of antidotes including pills and combinations of different vitamins and powders, fitting Rosa's description of what she refers to as the "pseudoscience-based recovery industry". And so while we tried so hard to prepare for what we had hoped would be a "soft landing", real life had a tendency of getting in our way.

At this time, my mother, living alone in the Midwest in an assisted living facility, suffered from sudden cardiac arrest. We had taken Mom back to Germany when she turned 80 and as a survivor of the Holocaust, she had suffered depression through most of her life. Our son read up about her community in Germany which had arranged for most of the Jewish population to be transported to Theresenstadt, where most of her family perished in the Nazi camp. It was a truly moving but profoundly sad trip for Mom as she recounted to me and my sister her years growing up under the Nazi regime. At age 18, she arranged to rescue her mother and father by purchasing tickets on the last ship allowed to leave Germany at the time for safe passage to America. I felt excitement and trepidation all at once, for I was apprehensive about taking her to her birthplace for her final visit, in honor of her 80th birthday. Though I tried to share these feelings with others, in my heart I truly felt that it was a rare gift that only a daughter of a survivor could understand. Our son read extensively about the small community in Bavaria, the Nazi occupation, and so much about the rise of the Third Reich that by the time we left to visit Germany in August, 2001, I felt comfortable with so much of his encyclopedic knowledge. His research was superb—thorough, historically accurate and relevant to our trip.

Of course, what was to come in the following months shattered our well-calculated plans for our son's smooth reentry back to Israel. Political upheaval such as what we experienced during the Intifada, a violent upsurge of Arab discontent, and 9/11 threw all of us into a state of high alert. This coupled with Mom's cardiac arrest and my trips to care for her, along with the challenges of helping him establish citizenship and a meaningful study program, and to allocate appropriate housing, filled the months following his return. Becoming an adult, we were to learn, was painstakingly slow, unpredictably complex and incredibly taxing for our son. It was also very hard on our family and the community in which we lived, for everyone was upset by the tension which invaded our lives during those horrible years of the Uprising or Second Intifada here in Israel. We knew that we could chart a course by observing and recording his growth and maturity. But what we did not know, no matter how hard we had worked to grasp this notion, was that bringing a thirty-something male on the spectrum back home was not only a huge step, but also one which had few distinct and familiar markings. We were just shooting in the dark as we tried to help him adjust to his new life. There was so much to prepare, so much to think about, and so little time and experience.

The quote by the late John Lennon that "Life is what happens when you are busy making other plans" is an expression that often came to my mind during those hectic, demanding and frustrating days. And so his becoming an adult was the next phase in our journey of trying to understand and affirm our son's rightful place in his new home. We did our best to enable our son to be himself or as he so well expressed it, "I am me." A walk gently into the light toward a meaningful life was our goal for our son. We became strengthened in spirit and in our hearts as we reached out to our community and found support, guidance, and care.

Chapter 7

An Uncertain Future

Our son was nearly thirty when events began to happen in our lives which somewhat confounded our abilities to deal with his condition and ever growing needs. Intellectually, we were knowledgeable about his recent diagnosis of Asperger syndrome. Emotionally, however, we were still in shock over the notion that our son—exceptionally verbal and articulate, logical, handsome and strong—could be autistic. We felt stuck in the classical Kanner model of what an autistic person is supposed to look like, and how one on the spectrum is expected to behave. Though our readings about the Asperger syndrome diagnosis were ongoing, and we concentrated on an analysis of the disorder, including diagnosis, interventions and early childhood development, the literature focused primarily, though not exclusively, on young children. The few exceptions were those describing troubled adolescents who had not yet joined the adult world.

A Lucky Man: Donald T.

One superbly written piece entitled "Autism's First Child" appeared in *The Atlantic* in October 2010. Well documented by authors John Donovan and Caren Zucker, it is the true story of a Mr. Donald Triplett of Mississippi, aged

77 at the time of the publication of the story, and according to records I have uncovered, still alive today and living in his family home in Mississippi.

For a number of years, there have been many moments when I have returned to this piece of journalism seeking direction, understanding, and a hypothetical outline of what may be in store for our son over the next few decades. It is an article well worth multiple readings both for its unique approach to the subject as well as its insights into the mysterious and nearly uncharted world of the adult autistic.

Donald Triplett, was the first child ever diagnosed with autism. Identified in the annals of autism as Case #1, Donald T. was the subject of a medical article written in 1943 announcing the discovery of a condition which had never been previously reported. At that time, the disorder was considered extremely rare, limited to Donald and ten other children. Over 75 years have passed since this first case. Since that time, the rate of diagnosis, as we know, has spiraled.

Over subsequent years, the scientific literature updated Donald's story, but about forty years ago, the narrative came to an abrupt halt. The authors raised the question: Whatever happened to Donald T.? They began searching for information and were able to locate some answers in documents filed away in the archives of Johns Hopkins. However, most of the answers came from Donald T. himself. This happened when Donovan and Zucker visited him in Forest, Mississippi, the same place where he had been living when the authors wrote about him in *The Atlantic* so many years before then.

This important article was a timely contribution to the field, as it grapples with the major questions that parents of adult children on the spectrum are faced with: What will happen to our children when we die? How will we be able to support their lives, after our passing, so that they are meaningful, independent and enriched? And are there systems in place, such as mental health care facilities, which can ease the burdens of the aging autistic adult?

These crucial issues and questions haunt me, and nearly every other parent of an adult child on the spectrum, on a daily basis. In fact, I believe that it was the urge to seek answers to these burning questions that motivated me to spend years researching and writing this book.

Adults on the Spectrum: Singing in a Different Key

Levels of anxiety and sources of stress need to be examined in a way which addresses the needs of the adult with autism. In the *Journal of Intellectual Disabilities*, the authors of a research article, Gillott and Standen, compare more than 30 adults with autism with 20 adults with intellectual disabilities using informant-based stress and anxiety measures. The conclusion of the study indicates that adults with autism were almost 3 times more anxious than the control group. Subscales of anxiety of panic, agoraphobia, separation anxiety and obsessive compulsive disorder (OCD) along with generalized anxiety disorder (GAD) were significantly higher. Overall, it was reported that the adults with autism were found to have higher stress from nearly all sources particularly in terms of their abilities to cope with change. The more anxious the person with autism was, the less likely they were able to cope. According to the authors, there is a growing and more significant body of evidence that cognitive behavioral interventions for the treatment and control of anxiety, for both adults and children, can be successful for those on the spectrum.

In a well-written and succinct summary of collaborative research presented in the Autism Organization of the UK report published in September 2016, intended for professionals in the field of autism research, Cos Michael pinpoints the major issues surrounding health care for the adult autistic community. The main question posed was: what are some discernable barriers to health care experienced by autistic adults compared with those without spectrum disorders? Not surprisingly, the results indicated that the autistic participants identified different and greater barriers to health care especially in areas related to patient-service provider communications, sensory perceptions and navigating through the health care system maze. Topping the list was fear and anxiety, cost related issues, and concern about not being able to process information in a way which would facilitate discussions with caregivers. In their conclusions, the researchers suggested that healthcare providers on many levels become more aware of perceived barriers as described by adults on the spectrum. They are in the process of finding ways to ease them, including direct interventions. The need to eliminate obstacles to the provision of health care is one area which calls out for greater sensitivity, increased awareness, and more meaningful responses. Only then can the discomfort experienced by the aging autistic facing inevitable health issues—including diabetes, elevated levels of cholesterol and blood pressure, and other age-related conditions—be alleviated.

I am reminded of an encounter we had several years ago with a well-known and respected lawyer living in our community. We decided that the time had come to establish a legal framework which will provide the resources our son might need for the remainder of his life. With a certain smugness and hubris, the lawyer turned to me and told me that while I could control and manage these issues as long as I am alive, there was no way to set up a legal system to guarantee that he would be appropriately looked after since I would no longer be around to oversee this. It was as though planning ahead for our son was, in his legal opinion, out of bounds and out of the question. However, at our insistence and following our clear instructions, he went on to prepare a last will and testament which, in fact, did address the needs of our son after our demise. A very strange encounter indeed.

Doctors often shy away from approaching a patient who is terminally ill as they are trained to cure, not to deal with issues of mortality. Similarly, it appears that lawyers are also uncomfortable in a situation as complex as crafting a formal document to provide a legal framework guaranteeing lifetime support for a disabled adult child with AS. I cannot emphasize enough how crucial this legal planning is for the sake of our children, when we as parents are no longer alive. Sadly, this vital issue is so often overlooked, and AS adults are left behind with no provisions made for their future.

Donovan, whose brother-in-law is on the spectrum, and Zucker, whose twenty-one year old son has autism, are affiliated with the ABC network. Donovan, a news reporter, and Zucker, a former ABC producer, recently published a book entitled *In a Different Key* which presents an overview of the history of autism, beginning and ending with the story of Donald T. (described earlier in this chapter). In a January, 2016 radio interview conducted on the Laurie Lynn Show on WILK Newsradio, both Donovan and Zucker explain the title of their new release. The word "key" does not refer to the physical key which fits into a lock but to the musical term. The authors allude to the notion that not every person does or should sing in the same musical key and singing in a different key should also be just fine.

They described their visits to Donald T, age 83, still a resident of a small rural community in Mississippi, whose life of independence and small pleasures deserve our respect and attention. In a sense, for them, Donald T. is the ultimate success story of one whose initial early diagnosis would have meant an empty life of someone doomed to be institutionalized. Against all odds, however, Donald has been very fortunate to have the family's commitment, passion, and financial resources to obstruct this fate. Thus, he enjoys a rich life as he goes about his daily activities which also include the occasional golf game and travel.

In the interview, Zucker touches upon the problem of children growing up into adulthood, in an environment which is totally unprepared to facilitate their entry into this stage in life. She describes a dismal scene of communities lacking critical and vital support services including housing and medical accessibility. As the population transitions, she notes, society as a whole and communities, specifically, must begin to address what the future holds for this growing but dependent population. Donald's life turned out "so well", claim the writers, that in a sense, they refer to him as a model for the best-case scenario—what really should be happening to adults on the spectrum. Until society is willing to recognize these needs, however, the future looks bleak, a topic I will attempt to examine in my final chapter of what lies ahead for our adult autistic children.

An interesting nexus of a meeting between Donald's family and Leo Kanner is well- documented in Silberman's comprehensive, recently published book on autism entitled *Neurotribes: The Legacy of Autism and the Future of Neurodiversity*. Interestingly enough, all three of the aforementioned authors—Silberman, Donovan and Zucker—chose Donald as an exemplary case to focus on in their writings. They all regard Donald as the first autistic to be identified (according to Kanner's diagnosis), and they describe his treatment, his life and where he is today. Kanner had assumed that Donald was doomed to a dismal future, and while not forthright in suggesting institutionalization, he offered little solace to the desperate family seeking a proper place in their Mississippi community. Kanner continued to consult with the family after his first meeting, where he noted in his records the word "schizophrenia" with a question mark. Kanner kept

Donald under observation for two weeks after which he was returned home from his visit at Johns Hopkins.

Four years following Kanner's first visit with the family, he wrote Donald's mother that he had encountered eight other children who exhibited similar characteristics—lack of interest in people, object fixation, desire to be left alone and fear of change. He advised them that in searching for a way to describe this condition, he wished to speak of it as an "autistic disturbance of affective contact". In fact, Kanner did not coin the term "autistic" as it was already in use in psychiatry, not as the name of a syndrome, but as an observational term describing a symptom rather than an illness. In September, 1942 he used this expression when corresponding with Mary Triplett, and one year later, he described Donald and eleven other children in his book *The Nervous Child*. At the same time, the Austrian physician, Hans Asperger, applied the word "autistic" to the behaviors he was seeing amongst the children in his care in the Austrian clinic. Yet the term "Asperger syndrome" remained largely unknown until it was translated from the German in the early 1990s.

The Tripplet family had much in their favor as they searched for ways to "cure" Donald of his affliction, as it was known at the time. They were a respected, prosperous family that was well-connected and admired by their community. After Donald had gone through a brief stint in an institution as a child, they decided to create their own safe haven and in so doing, set a standard for others. The precedent his family set is indeed helpful as we attempt to deal with adults on the spectrum, especially in regards to issues of aging, hospitalization, employment and housing. As if to underscore the lack of interest in trying to understand and support other patients, the facility in rural Mississippi where Donald Triplett lived for a year treated his case in a way that was totally unprofessional. When the family requested a written assessment of Donald's time in his facility and under his care, the director wrote less than half a page, concluding that their five year old boy's problem was probably some "glandular disease".

Essentially, the Triplett family carved out a niche for their son which included pleasurable routines such as weekly dinners with his sibling and leisurely activities including his own version of playing golf, as well as an irrevocable trust fund set up by the family to pay his expenses and a level of independence enabled by home care and supervision. But, as the authors of the article note, with all the strides Donald Triplett has made in his life, conversing appropriately was an act that still eludes him. The give and take of normal, everyday conversation was something Donald is simply incapable of delivering. In describing his mother's death when he was 52, it was clear to the authors that engaging in discussion which normally would stir empathy or emotions was difficult for Donald. His response to the circumstances of losing both his parents was rather detached and matter-of-fact, although he did admit missing them both.

His life today is based on a routine of activities and dominated by an intense desire to travel and see the world, albeit on his terms, and carefully planned with the help of a community travel advisor. His vacations in foreign countries are limited to just six days. He assembles photo albums based on his travels, and when he returns home, he busies himself planning his next trip abroad. In adulthood, Donald has developed a life of quiet acceptance by his neighbors in his small hometown of Forest, Mississippi. He is surrounded by people who knew him as a child and willingly accepted him into their community, while acknowledging that he is different from them.

Almost condemned to wither away in an institution, Donald was fortunate to have a family that refused to accept advice when they consulted with medical professionals. Instead, they chose a different route for their son, one filled with security, comfort and warm acceptance of an individual who is so different from them. Stability, predictability and security were part of the environment in which he was able to develop and grow into a respected though obviously odd member of his community. By the time his Mother died, Donald had matured and learned more about the world in which he was living and his place in it—much more than Mary Triplett could ever have imagined during those frightening early years of his childhood.

Coming Home

And so when our son packed up his bags, literally as well as metaphorically, to return to be close to our family in Israel, we knew that the challenges we would face would be varied. But what we did not know nor were we prepared for was just how frustrating and demanding and complicated they would be.

Looking at his strengths and interests as a young man struggling to become a responsible adult, we decided to try out different approaches to finding a niche for him in his new community. Our son's interest and curiosity about religion led us to consider enrolling him in several Yeshivot, or Jewish centers of learning, located throughout Jerusalem. This journey led us to places open only to older men with families, as well as residential types of learning institutions designed to meet the needs of those young men headed toward advanced religious studies. In addition, since our son had performed so well academically in college, we considered enrolling him in a Master's program at the Hebrew University for overseas students.

Both the world of academia and the Yeshiva seemed like good options to enable him to adjust to his new surroundings as each provided a reasonably safe haven in terms of support and a sense of dignity and purpose.

His academic studies went reasonably well, but as we should have realized, in retrospect, we did little to prepare the people with whom he interacted on a regular basis. They did not realize that a person with Asperger syndrome could act in ways which may appear to be threatening and unsettling. Our son researched and presented many papers relating to his courses and, according to his professors, did well in terms of content and comprehension of his subjects. He eagerly prepared for his courses, spending untold hours in the university library, attending classes, and turning in his assignments while receiving extensions due to what was described in his entrance application as a learning disability.

At the time, we were aware of his AS diagnosis but were not adequately knowledgeable about just how much this affected the learning environment in terms of his social behavior. We knew that he did not attend gatherings at the university set up to encourage students to get to know one another, nor did he go on the field trips which were part of his program. Somehow, we missed the point that while research assignments challenged, excited and interested him, any activities which involved social engagements with his peers, he simply avoided. So while we had immersed ourselves in learning more and more about AS, we simply failed to connect the dots leading to the obvious – any type of encounter which required social skills was very frightening and so overwhelming to him that he just declined to participate. He withdrew more and more although he seemed to derive great pleasure from his research and his studies.

Blaming a Harmless Man

And then came the inevitable snag. One day we received a telephone call from the security department at the university demanding that we come to an urgent meeting. I was visiting my sickly mother at the time, but the message conveyed to my husband was that our son was being suspended on the grounds of misconduct toward a female university staff person. After hours of negotiations, meetings, telephone conversations and face to face discussions, and many days later, an agreement was reached so that our son could finish the semester but that would end his university association. We had the delicate task of trying to explain to him that he would be unwelcome in the very place that had given him such comfort. He could no longer go to seminars, attend lectures nor use the library but he could write his final papers without physically attending classes.

The university security people simply demonstrated a lack of sensitivity and an unwillingness to recognize the diversity of a student population. Perhaps at that time it was expecting too much from a university department tasked with the job of protecting a specific population, but certainly those in positions of higher authority could have been keener to play a decision-making role when determining responsibility. To accuse one on the spectrum of inappropriate behavior is pitiful, and I can only hope that now, a decade later, the university is doing a much better job of understanding students singing in "different keys". I cannot understate the trauma, pain and sadness this action of throwing our son out of the university caused him. I can only hope that today, given the increased awareness about the behaviors of those suffering from an autism spectrum disorder, this university would be more accepting and tolerant. I am aware that they have worked on projects of accessibility for those university attendees who have severe physical handicaps. I do hope that future projects will also take into account those with mental disabilities, including those on the spectrum.

It was such a painful and sad time in our lives and in his life. How could he possibly understand that his infraction which, we later learned, took place during an elevator ride, when his inept attempt to start a conversation with a female worker was so horribly misinterpreted as an aggressive act, could lead to his immediate dismissal? We considered countercharging the accusations made by the security department. But in the end, we decided it was in our son's best interest to let go and move on, which we did as the Yeshiva opened its doors to him and welcomed him into their house of learning.

I recently read about a new initiative here in Israel of opening up an academic center, a university, specifically designed for those on the autism spectrum. While I applaud such an effort, it seems to me to be misguided. What is needed is inclusion, not exclusion. We need to welcome this population into the university setting rather than separating them out for special treatment. I think that we should all be well beyond the days of separate but equal treatment, but perhaps I am just more impatient as I approach my seventh decade!

Chunking Mundane Activities

And so, by default, good luck and good timing, our son attended the Yeshiva study program where he enthusiastically dove into his studies with a group of incredibly dedicated and kind rabbis and scholars. He loved the discussions he had with his teachers and enjoyed his acceptance into an environment which was nonjudgmental, intellectual and friendly. During his university years, he had lived at home but when he went into the Yeshiva world, we found him an apartment near ours so we could have daily contact with him. We were able to oversee his apartment, keeping it tidy and uncluttered. We tried not to get upset when, rather than using his one walk-in closet for clothes, he chose to hook up his computer in the closed space and spent many happy hours there. We made sure that he had good food, working appliances, and a reasonable standard of cleanliness. We hired a person to clean his apartment on a regular basis, which also meant throwing out the many loaves of bread that our son had collected in his freezer.

Each season, we went through his clothes, discarding, with his approval, things no longer in good condition. As I had an office in the city at that time, I hired him to clean it weekly in exchange for a salary reasonable enough for him to buy his own groceries. That went well until one night, he came into our home visibly shaken and upset. After calming him down, he told us that the manager of the local supermarket had shouted and threatened him, demanding that he leave. His crime was that he was taking up too much time, going from aisle to aisle trying to decide what to buy. Enraged by such mistreatment, my husband went to the supermarket and confronted the manager. After my husband explained our son's condition, the manager apologized profusely, inviting him to return with the promise that he would be welcomed and even given special assistance with his food purchases.

In both events, the university expulsion and the supermarket incident, had we prepared the authorities in advance, would this perhaps have made a difference? But, the question which haunts me is: how could we have known? In fact, an existential question troubles me nearly each day: How can I, the mother of an autistic son, chunk every mundane activity into some understandable piece to help smooth his path, to give him insights to guide and support him, and to keep him out of harm's way? I fully understand that failures are part of the fabric of living, that misunderstandings are often the result of poor communication, and that with laughter comes tears. But somehow, with an intensity and perseverance that is hard to describe, I feel the need to engage in a passionate and silent discussion with my son's interlocutors: I am me, understand who I am and why I am doing what I am doing, accept me as I am, and include me in your life.

To further emphasize the unfair stigmatization with which AS individuals are treated by society at large, some researchers have pointed out the fine line between genius and disability. For example, Kimberly Stephens and Joanne Ruthsatz recently wrote an article in the Opinion Section of the *NY Times* in which they describe some confusion about the overlap of the concept of prodigy and autism. Is the 18-month-old child who is capable of reciting the alphabet backwards destined for a diagnosis of autism, even though there is no blood test or genetic screening for either the child prodigy or the child on the spectrum? The mystery of just what autism is, they suggest, might be combined with a better understanding of what defines prodigy and in the case of the autistic, better and earlier diagnosis might pave the way for more effective treatment. In describing a characteristic which might blur the identity of the Asperger syndrome child with the prodigy, such as a passion for their particular subject of interest, the authors suggest that quite possibly prodigies may have a specific form of autism, a conjecture, they note, that is still unproven. They do however, state unequivocally that a possible connection between autism and prodigy is yet unproven and warn that their intention is not to give "false hope" to parents. And why should they worry?

Obviously, the stigma of an autistic diagnosis, one might conclude from this article, should not be confused with the identity of having raised a child prodigy. Stephens and Ruthsatz hypothesize that child prodigies may have been at risk of developing autism but did not, a connection awaiting research. But this begs the question, in my opinion. The tone of the article seems to suggest that while prodigies are viewed with great admiration and awe, the autistic diagnosis is a life sentence. For example, brain disorders are a focus of studies by the National Institutes of Health (NIH). So rather than helping the reader to appreciate their potential strengths and contributions to society, once again, we are faced with a situation in which conjecture, nuance and implication suggest that the brain of one on the spectrum awaits scientific investigation and explanation rather than understanding, compassion and acceptance. Unlike the child prodigy, they imply, the child on the spectrum remains a mystery and a curiosity rather than a cultural asset. Sad, indeed.

In addressing the Third Annual Day of Learning sponsored by the Autism Science Foundation in April, 2016, Dr. Gerald Fischbach presented a talk on autism entitled "Where Are We Now?" in a brilliant and informative manner. Dr. Fischbach concluded his presentation, which focused on synapses and scientific advances, with the comment that despite all the impatience for some revolutionary changes in the research, the goal still remains to make the lives of those with the autistic spectrum condition "more livable". His compassionate call echoes that of so many parents whose goal for their adult child is to lead them toward a meaningful life.

And so while our son was busy becoming an adult, a certain rhythm began to surface, the musical key was emerging, and we as a family began to come to terms with the reality that our child had transitioned to adulthood. With that passage, came obligations, responsibilities, and a new and challenging reality.

Thirty-Something and Still Stumbling

It was a critical period in our son's life. He was in his mid-thirties, a time when many young males become more settled into some type of domestic situation, work responsibilities, and routine which might define who they are becoming through their relationships, parenthood and employment. Neither scenario was realistic or attainable for our son during the early years of 2000. He was searching, introverted, frustrated, and unhappy. Discontented with what he perceived as a life of failures and disappointments, he turned to the only safe haven he could find to express his anger and pain—the family.

As his parents, those years following his disastrous encounters at the university were torturous, as we attempted to define his persona in terms of his condition. We struggled to make sense of and forgive his angry outbursts directed at us on a regular basis. Fortunately for him and for us, our other two children were busily forging ahead, defining their lifestyles and identities through army service, global travels, and university studies, precisely those areas that were unavailable at the time to someone on the spectrum.

And so we began to search for some measure of community support and services. I remember how livid I was with my accountant when she unwisely suggested that my family might be eligible through the web of social services for financial assistance and support. I explained to her with great patience and emotion that my son was my responsibility, not the responsibility of the state. I told her thank you very much, but we would continue to provide for his needs.

After endless months of anguish and fear, we began to understand that we could not continue on our own. We realized that, yes, while we assumed full responsibility for our son's wellbeing, we were not in this by ourselves, nor did we have answers to unspoken questions. We had to admit that we were no longer certain that we could keep him from some form of institutionalization. His outbursts were becoming more frequent and violent. He seemed so sad and melancholy that at times, we just wanted to hold him, to comfort him, and to promise him that things would work out just fine, reassurance we as parents truly questioned.

And so chance encounters opened doors to us we had not considered in the past. We began to realize that we needed medical, legal, and emotional support, and this took expression by seeking out help from friends, family, associates and neighbors in our community. Gradually, we opened up to the notion that our family was in distress. With our insights and new voice, we sought legal advice and it became increasingly clear that our son was eligible for financial assistance in the form of rental subsidies, training for employment, and additional services. Before I attended a hearing at the local office for social services, I was warned that the interviewing board was typically not empathic, and that they could be harsh, nasty, and unkind. The board hearing took place in a simple room attended by a panel of doctors, social workers, and administrative personnel.

Undaunted, I actually looked forward to telling them my whole story. My son was in attendance according to the laws of the state. The hearing was rather banal until they asked about employment. Absolutely stunned, my son was unable to articulate the history of his past occupations or his future interests in developing employable skills. They were direct and repetitive, but after some time, they turned to me to ask how a thirty-year-old could get to the point of being so dependent on his parents. That was the moment when I explained, thoughtfully, carefully and with little emotion, that given my son's diagnosis and condition, I would be willing to pay any sum of money to take him anywhere in the world, if they could just recommend a suitable venue. I then turned to them and asked if they knew of such a place where my son could be "cured of his 'affliction'". I guess this was the turning point, as the tone suddenly changed from anger and disrespect to one of compassion as they understood my sadness and pain. They declared that he was eligible to receive subsidies and services, provided by the state, for a lifetime.

It was time to investigate exactly what the state could make available to my Asperger son. This was the start of another chapter in his life, one which was filled with greater optimism and hope. It was now loud and clear, and legal and even ok. The state understood and heard the voice of a desperate mother whose only goal was to find the right path for her child on the spectrum.

Subsequent hearings took place over several months, most of which were bureaucratic and mundane. We navigated our way through the network of services for which he was deemed eligible, ultimately reaching a local service care provider for adults with a variety of disabilities called Shekel, Community

Services for People with Special Needs. Their offices are headquartered in Jerusalem, under the competent and compassionate leadership of its CEO, Clara Feldman.

The Turning Point: A More Hopeful Future

My first visit to the training center introduced me to their approach of how to meet the needs of the disabled population. I explained how I had found them and what my goals were, although I was somewhat apprehensive that the polite, well-trained senior case worker would react with annoyance or at best, frustration, with my rather aggressive and demanding approach. So I was pleasantly startled when he responded that I had every right to advocate for my son's best interest, and that as a parent of a disabled adult child, that was not only my responsibility but also my obligation. We met and spoke regularly for several months as they began the process of initiating him into their network of services. For me, it was a period of great expectations, undimmed hope, and unheralded optimism, feelings which today, over a decade later, I still experience when speaking about this agency and committed staff, including Offer Dahary, the deputy director who was my son's initial contact. In time my son came to look upon Offer as a friend and mentor.

Back then, our son was still living in a small studio apartment near our home, attending the Yeshiva, and spending far too much time being angry with us about nearly everything. I wondered what was worse— having him far away and emotionally distant, or close by and the easy target of his anger for all that had gone awry in his life. But slowly and methodically, we came to terms with his condition and just what that meant for a young adult seeking his own identity in a society overburdened with security and financial constraints.

Each step toward helping him, and by extension, his parents, to discover and reach greater independence and familial and societal acceptance was challenging, if not arduous. But we moved forward, promoting his case, strengthening family ties and connections, while at the same time, benefitting from the ongoing support our service care provider Shekel offered. For the first time since our son was a young child diagnosed with learning disabilities and dyslexia, we felt that we were encircled by a support network that was professional in its approach, unconditionally empathic and nonjudgmental. We found a safe community for our son, comprised not only of our family, but also friends and work colleagues who knew him and accepted him for what he was. He literally became who he is and who he had been all the time. As one expert in autism remarked, the condition was actually always there.

By now, of course, we knew all too well how he would react negatively and even become verbally abusive when he was confronted with any change. Over time and with good therapy and support, he is more accepting and tolerant of shifts in employment or other arrangements. Since we had always insisted that he be mainstreamed during his elementary and high school years, he could mirror and model acceptable behaviors; we applied this same thinking to his work opportunities. After several upsetting failures, he was given a mentor or shadow who could help him to learn new skills such as accounting and administrative tasks. After a relatively short time, his sharp intellect seemed to click in and he was able to achieve job independence, completing his work assignments in a timely manner.

He was also invited to work as an aide in a therapeutic pool for the severely disabled. He travels many miles from his apartment to go to this pool and to assist the therapists as they exercise the participants, helping them with aquatic activities. He is loved by the people whom he helps and contributes to their sense of well-being by always being friendly, helpful and with a good sense of humor. In college, he had mastered several computer programs which enabled him to complete his written assignments. Transferring these skills to accounting came quite easily to him as he acquired the skills necessary to support his current work assignment in the offices of the agency which is also his service provider. In addition, he serves as an administrative assistant, doing the more menial administrative tasks so many people shy away from, for example, making copies, answering the phones, running routine errands such as going to the post office, and other duties.

He enjoys the daily challenges and takes his responsibilities very seriously, sometimes even assuming authority which he doesn't actually have, but enjoys exercising when he thinks it is important. The entire staff was so pleased as well as amused when during the Gaza War in 2014, he posted a sign outside the offices advising personnel to return home as we were under threat of missile attacks. It was true, but life went on as usual and he learned that even under dire circumstances, people must continue to live with as much normalcy as possible.

In order to help get his building ready for the impending war, he took upon himself the responsibility of clearing out the community bomb shelters and posting signs, advising neighbors where to go when they heard the sirens. Diagnosed with one of the most debilitating conditions, our son acted with courage, fortitude and determination as he eagerly gave of himself, rather than passively waiting for help to arrive when there was a threat of attack. And so this sense of self, his willingness to take action and to be a useful and productive member of his community is what gives us a feeling of optimism. All we can hope for is that his life will continue as it is now — enriched by his acts of good deeds and his acceptance into the tough and demanding Israeli society in which he lives today.

The Case of the Leaking Pipe

We strive toward establishing a system or network of services available to support his desire to live independently while continuing to work in the offices of the agency which oversees his daily activities. His ongoing need for support and assistance is now accepted by both him and us as simply another way of living a full and enriched life. We are always, nonetheless, vigilant as we are acutely aware of just how quickly minor events can spiral downward, causing utter chaos. For example, a leak in the bathroom pipe was solved by our son by wrapping the bundles of dry towels around the pipe, a rather clever solution to the problem, but clearly, neither permanent nor safe. Eventually, the leak dripped into the apartment of his neighbor below him, a rather sully single woman who called us one night to come see what damage such a drip had caused. She claimed that she had told our son about this situation weeks earlier (which was probably true), but she missed the point that he had absolutely no clue how to solve the issue of the dripping pipe. It was rather difficult to convince him of the need for a plumber, as he preferred to just wring out the towels, replace them with dry ones, and continue to wrap the pipe.

It was an important lesson for him to learn, however, that sometimes what may appear to be a logical, reasonable, and clever solution, does not always work, in spite of his best efforts. And recognizing the need for help and seeking out appropriate resources was a lesson both we, as his parents, and he, in his fourth decade, are learning to accept as one of life's challenging realities. The issue of the dripping pipe, then, became a metaphor for his sometimes comic, sometimes exasperating, and otherwise temperamentally autistic approach to life and the challenges it presents.

A similar drama played out regarding the need to heat the apartment and to make hot water available to him. After futile attempts at explaining that the air conditioner could be used as a heating system by simply switching the monitor into heat mode and the water heated up by the flick of an electric switch, we gave up. To placate him, we decided to install a new heating system which could deliver warmth by using old and rusty radiators. The details and effort that went into the installation, servicing and replacing old, rusty plumbing are simply too numerous to write about but after months of negotiations, finding trained and reliable service people and installing a good heating system, today his place is cozy and warm and the hot water is plentiful. He actually found the solution for regulating the system by installing a timer. That way, the decision to turn the system on and off was determined by setting the clock, rather than him worrying about when and for how long he would need to heat the apartment and his water.

When his dryer malfunctioned, he contacted the appliance department as we had signed a contract enabling him to use their services. In addition, we recently purchased a new stove for his kitchen which was user-friendly. We were thus able to convince him that his need for backups in the form of multiple microwaves and toaster ovens were no longer necessary and after some coaxing, he agreed to pack up and store the three microwaves and two toaster ovens he had accumulated over time. Once he was satisfied that the heating system would work continuously, he also agreed to put away the portable air conditioning and heating units which were stored in closets throughout his little apartment. In addition, he understands very well and accepts the need for ongoing home inspections to prevent any health or fire hazards. In fact, at least one week each month, along with the assistance of his home aid, he busily sorts through items he has managed to collect and gets rid of them, so that the inspector approves the status of his apartment. His home aid, a kind and thoughtful young musician who comes to our son's apartment each week for up to six hours, speaks about how much fun they have cooking, planning menus and organizing his home to make it more comfortable. Making lives "more liveable" as Dr. Fischbach commented in his Day of Learning presentation is indeed an ongoing challenge and goal.

The Best Scrambled Eggs Ever

An older colleague friend maintains my son's computer and is readily available whenever he needs technical support. This kindly gentleman, born in Germany, is a volunteer for the nonprofit agency where he works side-by-side with my son as they upgrade, maintain, and repair the systems. My son also works in the accounting department, sorting out the receipts which aid in setting up budgets for the apartments under the aegis of the organization.

Recently we were told that our son's current position in accounting may become redundant and thus, he would no longer be of use to this department. After months of meetings with his team, including the psychologist, counselor and guides, we came up with a strategy to enable him to transition from accounts to the "leisure time" department which provides opportunities for clients to travel, participate in community events such as musical performances and other cultural activities. This department is tasked with organizing, supervising and funding a variety of activities to enrich the disabled adult population they serve. Our son is very capable of translating from Hebrew to English, accounting, organizing tours, and researching background information for various destinations. He will soon be given training for his integration into this very special and important department, with the help of a work mentor or coach to guide, supervise and instruct him in all the necessary details of his new position. We know how challenging this will be for him, but we all believe that he is ready. He is clearly very capable of moving forward to another level which may give him greater self-confidence and respect, prestige and a better sense of his capacity to achieve. His potential is unquestionable and with the encouragement of his work peers, family and support team, we believe that he can succeed. In addition, we recruited the former head of the psychology division of the Ministry of Education, a retired professional and lifelong family friend, to act as his mentor as he transitions into another stage of employment.

We are now more optimistic as we appreciate just how much he has matured and adapted to the many challenges faced by an individual on the spectrum. On the day that the new stove we purchased for him was delivered to his apartment, he invited me to eat scrambled eggs he was preparing. These were the best scrambled eggs I have ever eaten! He prepared those eggs with a sense of genuine pride and joy, serving them to me with the sweetest grin I had seen in many years!

And now, looking back at the debilitating characteristics which inform an autistic spectrum diagnosis – lack of interest in people, object fixation, desire to be left alone and fear of change, I can say with some degree of certainty that while these characteristics may, in fact, still surface under stressful and anxiety-provoking circumstances, he somehow manages to override these natural inclinations. It is definitely a step in the right direction, for in the past these negative traits were once so dominant in his life that they controlled his actions and threatened to seal his destiny.

Today, he is a forty-plus man, proud of his work, fascinated by his travels, intellectually curious, and mindful of his abilities and difficulties. He speaks about his family, his work associates and his neighbors with humor and acceptance which perhaps comes with maturity and a sense of belonging to a community who knows just who he is. Like the Donald T. journey, we can only hope that his life will be continuously enriched, driven by strong self-determination and commitment to live life to its fullest. He is, as he says, a work in progress, and has always been who he is today. As if to sum up his insights, he very often repeats the concise but poignant statement, "I am me".

CHAPTER 8

What Lies Ahead

Broken Promises

I am often so baffled when I read articles which seem to conveniently deny the fact that a population exists outside of what we now commonly refer to as the neurotypical community. Sometimes, the terminology used to depict this weak population is degrading, and this in turn exacerbates their status within their community. Just recently, an article in the English language edition of a highly respected newspaper here in Israel, *Haaretz*, caught my eye with the following headline "Court Rebukes State for Using Term 'Mental Retardation'". A case having to do with the placement in a residential community of a person described as having intellectual and developmental disabilities used the term in its ruling by the courts. As the article indeed pointed out, following a directive in June, 2012, the Ministry of Social Affairs reflected the change from "mentally retarded" to "persons with developmental and mental disabilities" by renaming one of its offices from the Division for the Mentally Retarded to the Division for Intellectual and Developmental Disabilities.

While literature in this ministry demonstrated this shifting of labels, it did not fulfill its promise to do so in the law. This oversight resulted in the state often using the term "mentally retarded" in some official documents and court proceedings. In this case, social mores were expected to drive and enshrine in the law that the demeaning and ugly term "mentally retarded" be struck from all legal documents. The current social affairs minister has requested that a specific amendment be drafted guaranteeing that this change in terminology be recognized and upheld.

The law continues to use these detrimental terms even though twenty years have passed since the legislative ruling unequivocally pronounced that the dignity of persons with disabilities must be protected under law. They had agreed back then that this population has the right to participate fully in society, as equals, in every sphere of life. Thus, this ruling issued over two decades ago, was based on the principle of equality and the recognition of the worth of every human being and the right of each person's dignity. In other words, the shift of the wording derives from the same duty to uphold human dignity although, as we see from this current case, the enforcement, even linguistically, lags sadly behind. The fundamental question in helping us parents craft and guarantee a secure future for our adult children is quite simple: Who will honor, protect, and respect the dignity of our children when we as parents, are no longer alive? In other words, what lies ahead for our children?

In dealing with these fundamental questions about what lies ahead for our children, it is crucial to address how their future is determined by us and upheld by the law. Choosing to become the lifelong custodian for an adult child on the spectrum, for example, is a very complicated and private decision.

According to studies conducted under Carol Povey's aegis of the National Autistic Society, some startling facts have emerged, including the revelation that almost half of the parents and siblings of adult autistic family members have not yet made any future plans for them. Noting this information reinforced my decision to have legal custodianship over my son which, when my husband and I are deceased, will become the responsibility of his siblings, under the supervision of the state judicial system. Nevertheless, according to this survey, 96% of these parents were worried about their child's future. Siblings of adults on the spectrum also see themselves as future caregivers though nearly half indicated that giving support to their autistic sibling might cause tension both to their families and to themselves, which is neither an unreasonable nor an unrealistic concern.

In one sense, for me personally, I felt that I was giving up all hope of my son achieving some degree of independence. I perceived custodianship as taking away his right to choose and his decision-making powers in all realms of his life. I felt that by taking a legal course of action, which dragged on for close to three years, I was betraying my son and denying him the right to achieve personal happiness in whichever way suited him. Ironically, it took the efforts of the judicial system including our legal representative to assure me that this was not at all the case. Only under specific circumstances would it be known that we had custodianship and these were well defined. While not going into the legal framework and details, suffice it to say that after fully understanding the short and long term implications of our decision, I was convinced that we were, in the end, doing the right thing. We were, in fact, paving the way for what may lie ahead for our son when we are no longer alive.

Misplaced and Misunderstood

Our family resides in a threatened and dangerous neighborhood and caution must be exercised on a daily basis. Living as we do in the turmoil and unpredictability of the Middle East, our immediate surroundings can sometimes be perceived as under constant threat. As citizens, we are in fact trained to be aware and suspicious. This hyper-vigilance of our environment, while sometimes life-saving, can quickly get out of hand. For example, when a person is asked to halt, show his or her identity papers or approach a police authority, an innocent gesture such as raising one's arms might be misconstrued as menacing. This erroneous interpretation can result in an overreaction, inadvertently, by an untrained person who is authorized to protect the public interest or someone who has no knowledge about persons that are different.

By taking custodianship of our son, we are shielding him from being misidentified. He now understands that he must have his identity card with him at all times and he must listen carefully to instructions when he is confronted by a member of the police force.

Custodianship is discretely recorded on his citizen identity card. In addition, he carries a card which categorizes him as disabled while not spelling out the exact nature of his limitations. His dignity and privacy, we feel, are protected while at the same time, ensuring his safety. We want to avoid a situation similar to one described in the May, 2016 article in *Haaretz* which reveals the fact that Israel apparently has no place for the mentally unfit when accused of a crime except for jail. In recent years, according to Public Defender Hagit Larnau, the number of indictments against persons with mental deficiencies is disproportionately high when compared to the number of mentally deficient people in any given community. Examples given were from populations in Canada and the US. In Canada, for example, the percentage of mentally deficient prisoners is between 5-10 percent, even reaching as high as 30 percent in some states in the US.

Statistics illustrate this unfortunate situation; the Israeli Public Defenders Office has noted that over the past five years, some 100 "mentally disturbed offenders" have been detained in jails. In this category were those adults diagnosed with ASD. The freedom to be seen in public and to interact with others under normal circumstances, such as shopping or riding a bus, are fundamental rights. We never question these, except when the individual is acting in a way that is perceived by others as strange or threatening. Indeed, this is where in Israel at least, the adult autism spectrum disorder individual lives, in a world of suspension - sometimes filled with subtle threats, often rejection and far too often, suspicion - a situation which may lead to possible imprisonment.

I am reminded of an interview with the authors of *In a Different Key: The Story of Autism,* John Donovan and Caren Zucker, who were mentioned in the previous chapter. In their newly published book, they relate a story that occurred on a public bus about a young adult man who began to exhibit some characteristics associated with ASD. Several passengers became concerned when they witnessed his seemingly agitated and weird behavior. As they got up to exit the bus, a couple nearby shouted out to the anxious passengers not to be concerned since clearly, the young man was autistic. With these words, the alarmed people relaxed, accepted this explanation, and continued on their way.

Donovan and Zucker suggest that this scenario is a metaphor indicating, perhaps, a better and brighter future for those on the spectrum. The stages of acceptance and inclusion in a neurotypical environment might be described as initial fear of the inexplicable behavior of the strangers in our midst. This is followed by awareness of the individual's condition, acceptance of his disability and ultimately inclusion in the community of people. And so, in a perfect world, where we find an enlightened population, our adult children can be assured of a safe and kind domain in which they can age with dignity and acceptance. Unfortunately, from the current literature about research and trends as reported by some of the most respected names in autism studies, we have to conclude that we still have a very long way to go. As summed up by one of the founders of the Knoxville Project Beth Ritchie, we have not yet created our own utopian world for our adult children on the spectrum.

His Dream...and Ours

But dream we must, while we continue building and developing healthy living options for our children. Of course, we have not yet reached the situation so poignantly envisioned by the late Dr. Martin Luther King in his immortalized speech in Washington, D.C. His touching "I Have a Dream" oration remains to this day, an expression of the hopes of a minority population that has been disenfranchised and belittled through the majority's actions and claims.

Delivered in the summer of 1963 at the Lincoln Memorial to crowds participating in the march for civil rights, he declared that he had a dream that his four little children will be judged not by the color of their skin, but rather by the "content of their character".

And our children, so different, so delicate, so precious and so often maligned and misunderstood, can pass the character content test possibly better than most human beings as we know that their natural disposition is toward giving not taking, kindness not cruelty, enlightenment not ignorance. Building on Martin Luther King's inspirational legacy and vision, our dream would be to provide appropriate responses to our children's housing, medical and social needs, which are now so sorely neglected.

A review of the literature about the aging population on the spectrum indicates a growing sense of awareness that, unfortunately, little thought or consideration has been given over the last millennium to the needs of this weak population. A recent editorial in the English version of the progressive newspaper *Haaretz* seemed to confirm our worst fears. Entitled "Abandoned by the State" the article paints a truly miserable picture of the housing situation of the 1,400 autistic men and women in Israel residing in nationwide hostels, defined as living quarters with up to four residents per unit. According to the author, responsibility for this population has been shifted from the state to NGOs and private organizations which receive funding to oversee the care of those on the spectrum. The issues presented in this scathing editorial include neglect, untrained workers, and no supervision. Some of these failures are a direct consequence of the minimal requirements of its staff: only twelve years of education and little to no preparatory training. Additionally, they receive minimum wages with a nearly 50% annual turnover.

Families who choose not to send their children to these hostels receive half of the sum which the state pays directly to those operating them, in a sense, punishing parents for keeping their autistic kids at home or in a family-owned or rented apartment. Notably, the editorial calls for the Israeli Social Affairs Ministry to review operational costs of the hostels while, at the same time, provisioning increased support for those with disabilities. Thus, they would be enabled to live independently in apartments while receiving necessary state supervision. In conclusion, this editorial states that it is indeed the responsibility of the State to provide funds, organization and supervision for whichever housing option families choose for the autistic population, who are "one of the weakest groups in Israeli society" and by extension, in most civil societies today.

The question, of course, remains: How does the natural process of aging, including vital issues such as appropriate housing, financial support, health care, and social needs, affect those adults diagnosed with autism? Carol Povey, Director of the Centre for Autism in the National Autistic Society, a registered charity in England, addresses these housing and related issues in her well documented article "Who Cares? Supporting Adults with Autism as They Get Older". In an effort to describe and define the needs of the adults on the spectrum, this center organized a campaign to help establish the Autism Act of 2009. The local authorities and health systems in England were thus mandated by law to properly plan and deliver services for adults with autism.

The commonly accepted "triad of impairments" relating to difficulties with communication, social imagination and interactions, continues to affect those on the spectrum throughout their lives. How this triad impacts their future as aging adults is still under investigation though, thankfully, it is now being looked at more seriously and more carefully. As noted earlier, recognizing the needs of this population is enshrined in the laws of many countries including Israel, the UK and the US. Unfortunately, however, scant attention has been given to how those needs might be both expressed by the individual on the spectrum and met by the local governmental authorities, including social services, health funds and charities.

There is some speculation, though largely based upon hope and anecdotal evidence, that as the adult population on the spectrum matures and the adaptation process deepens, there may be a decrease in the level of his or her disability. However, this does seem counterintuitive and perhaps, overly optimistic. Hilde Geurts, a neuropsychologist at the University of Amsterdam, investigated her observation in the clinic for autistic adults that many of the men and women appear to have depression. In a recently published study, she and her colleagues documented the prevalence of psychiatric disorders and symptoms in individuals between 55 and 79 years of age. An interesting finding was that psychiatric symptoms, as noted above, were less prevalent amongst the older adults with autism than the younger ones. The biggest discrepancy was with social anxiety which may indicate that, over time, adults with ASD develop tools to cope with social situations. This is an area that needs further investigation as the suggestion that time, exposure to social occasions, good modeling, and training in compensatory skills, including skill sets, can reduce the very deficiencies associated with Asperger syndrome and other autistic spectrum disorders. Certainly, regarding our son, we cling to the belief that social engagement in a supportive and understanding work environment combined with ongoing community and family support help to reduce his symptoms and the stigma of an adult condemned to live with the autistic diagnosis. I say "condemned" as a play on the observation that in existential terms, we are all, neurotypical and otherwise, indeed, condemned to live.

A Silver Lining: Happier Adults?

In an article presented by PubMed in February 2016, entitled "Psychiatric Co-occurring Symptoms and Disorders in Young, Middle-Aged, and Older Adults with Autism Spectrum Disorder," the authors indicate that psychiatric issues related to depression and anxiety appear to be less prevalent in older aged individuals with Autism Spectrum Disorders. This conclusion seems to confirm Geurts' hypothesis as well. Both studies and researchers indicate a trend that, over time and with good support systems, depression episodes and anxiety might in fact be lessened. This is clearly an assumption worth investigating through evidence-based studies, longitudinal research, and clinical observations.

Another article published in the August 2016 *Spectrum* series by Jessica Wright entitled "Never Mind Statistics: Adults with Autism May be Happy" suggests that, putting data and statistics aside, adults affected by the autism diagnosis may actually become more contented as they mature. While this population may not reach financial or personal milestones and independence, many appear to be satisfied with their lives. Wright points out that while persons with Asperger Syndrome are unable to actualize their full intellectual potential, we cannot jump to the conclusion that they are unhappy with their lives as adults on the spectrum. Despite their severe troubles functioning in everyday life, many in this study were able to achieve an impressive level of personal happiness. Quality of life, therefore, for the adult autistic population needs to be better defined in keeping with the limitations and restrictions which go along with the diagnosis; however, it is conceivable that they are indeed able to achieve a higher degree of contentment than had been previously reported.

These are hopeful first cues that this population, so long ignored, forgotten, or marginalized seem to be able to cope reasonably well as they age, indicating that the aging process becomes in a sense a level playing field. Much more research is needed to confirm this hypothesis, but it is not enough to wait for the research to inform important decisions regarding future needs of our adult children.

Developing support systems to help our children remain independent and healthy as they age is imperative. Established boundaries and sharing in the responsibility of looking after an aging sibling or citizen await our input and outcry. Social, economic and legal implications remain blurred. And so many critical issues facing this aging special population remain underestimated. Digby Tantam's studies, for example, paint a bleak picture of high unemployment, mental health issues such as anxiety and depression, and social rejection, much more so for the aged group suffering from autism than the general population. To say the least, this is a somewhat different picture than the one described earlier by Hilde Geurts and others.

The conflicting studies and data, missing information and lack of empirical data, have sadly resulted in very little advancement being made which could help this population as they age. Supports like adult day care centers, independent living facilities, and residential centers for the aging population do not include the autistic adult. These places have not made any special accommodations to meet their needs, a situation for the adult similar to the one that existed a decade earlier in the educational system for children. In other words, we see a parallel here of systems which are lacking way behind needs.

An informative article presented by the Autism Science Foundation entitled "Transitioning into Adulthood," describes the steps and circumstances ushering in the transition period, postsecondary school to adulthood. The Individuals with Disabilities Education Act (IDEA) mandates public education in most states for children from age 3-21. An Individual Education Program (IEP) specifies these requirements.

Our son, for example, had an IEP developed annually to guide his teachers as they made an effort to meet his goals and needs, taking into consideration his dyslexia and general learning disabilities. While it was a sincere attempt to define in more specific terms what was in his best interest in terms of learning styles and approaches, in actuality, it did little to enrich his learning environment. The special tools and compensatory skills he acquired were generally thanks to the private tutors we hired to help him absorb the information he received in the classroom. I do remember my struggles with the administration to keep him in his age appropriate class as he had developed a very supportive and healthy relationship with his peers. I rebuked the suggestions that he attend special classes as, at this point in his life, I felt that his social connectedness was just as important as his academic environment. This was an ongoing discussion with the administrative staff of his school in Maryland. Naturally, as he grew and faced untold challenges in other settings, my ability to protect him from isolation became more and more subdued. While an IEP, in my opinion, explicitly presented his learning strengths and deficits, it was not substantially supported by a teaching staff already overburdened by sheer numbers of students in the classroom. My experience was not very positive but this was thirty years ago and undoubtedly, much has changed in part, due to parent advocacy groups and a growing trend of awareness that neurodiversity exists among all ages in any given population.

The transition to adulthood includes employment training opportunities, post-secondary studies in universities and colleges, as well as housing options. Planning for this stage takes thought, care and experts to guide parents and maturing children as they make decisions which shape their futures.

Life is not so linear. While we may wish, as parents, to map out our child's future, clearly we cannot know what circumstances may arise which require rethinking and redirecting our energies and resources. As Steven Shapin describes so beautifully in a recent issue of *The New Yorker* in an article entitled "Seeing the Spectrum," the world as we know it is both disorderly and unpredictable. How we cope and accept, or deny and defy, our chaotic world greatly impacts our relationship with our universe.

The situation of the aging adult on the spectrum is far from clear. There are discrepancies, ambiguities, and contradictions which are further reinforced by the lack of coherent research. To my mind, the current research remains confusing, since on one hand, it points to a reduction in psychiatric issues among this population, and on the other hand, persons such as Tantam tend to paint rather bleak profiles. Are we to assume from the increased attention to adults on the spectrum that we can expect a fuller commitment to funding, research, and development from local authorities and governmental agencies? Can we hope that this will be followed by openness and willingness on the part of the general population to accept, embrace or at least tolerate in their communities those whose neurological wiring marks them as different? Are we to infer that with increased awareness, more education and enlightenment, someone who is different will not be judged as threatening and can become a full-fledged member of a civil society? Will the discourse accompanying such a shift be characterized by greater acceptance, kindness and sensitivity?

Indeed, there are people in my son's work and living community, often simple in manner and demeanor, who appear happy to accept him as the awkward person he is, without questioning his behavior and looking for solutions which might cause him to seem inferior. For that unconditional acceptance, I am relieved and grateful. My son is in his forties, generally a period when stability replaces restlessness and values engrained from childhood define the actions, beliefs and behaviors of the maturing adult.

But as the mother of a son with AS, I dwell upon what awaits him as we work so hard to secure a future which will be as safe, productive and fulfilling as possible. As I look ahead, I must also consider the present situation of this population in terms of housing options, as well as mental and general health issues. I realize that they will have to confront predictable struggles to thrive and forge a happy and healthy life style.

Sad Stories and Unfortunate Journeys

While autism was included in the Diagnostic and Statistical Manual of Mental Disorders in the 1980 edition, it was over a decade later, as pointed out in my earlier chapters, that the term Asperger syndrome appeared, only to be folded into the recent edition. The senior citizen of today was a child when the medical concept of an autistic spectrum disorder, as defined by Kanner in the early 1940s, was recognized by the medical community. In the past, or so it seems, autism went unnoticed, or if it was suspected, the young child was often condemned to live out a miserable life in a cold and uncaring institutional setting.

Thinking ahead, I must also remember past struggles and confrontations as they help guide our current interest and ability to make informed decisions about critical issues. During an interview, Peter Moscariello, the father of two young male adults on the spectrum, suggested that his boys may be the "pioneer generation" for children on the autism spectrum. In a touching article, both parents depict in vivid and familiar detail, the journey they have been on since their sons were diagnosed. "Dead ends, many…dead ends" is the way Peter's wife May describes their often desperate search for appropriate educational options for their older son, Michael. Phone calls to doctors, researchers, insurance providers, and other parents took up much of their time as they tried to find solutions for their son's ever-growing needs. Graduating at age 22 from the high school where his father was head of the math department, Michael credits the support of his one friend, Dave, for believing in him, and in his eyes, even saving his life.

Susan Parish, a professor of disability policy at Brandeis University, describes the tough situation now faced by the Moscariello family. A federal law, the Individuals with Disabilities Education Act, requires that schools provide appropriate services for all students, including those who have disabilities, until they are 22. Sadly, however, after that age, adult services simply do not exist. Their son now lives alone in an apartment partially subsidized by the city and state and receives food stamps and Medicaid. As the parents are in their mid-60s, they describe a situation of worrying who will keep an eye on their son. Parish explains that the search for lifelong support has been futile as entitlement to services is nonexistent for adults on the spectrum in the U.S. Emphasizing the gap in providing critical needs for this disabled population, Parish describes it as facing a "dead end." May declares that her autistic young sons are not to be blamed, instead, she declares, that her children were "crushed socially, by the world", a profoundly sad perception of the current state of affairs. The Moscariello family is certainly making a legitimate claim, and they have every right to be resentful. Services today for the diagnosed child with ASD may start earlier, the specific needs of the child with autism may be met, but, what happens when this population reaches the age of 23 and beyond? That is the question faced by so many families, like this one and my own.

The story of the Moscariello family, for example, reminds me about how so little information can disrupt a family. I read with deep consternation stories similar in tone to their sad journey like the one penned in 2011 by Deborah Rudacille, describing the elderly who were diagnosed late in life and, sadly, remain as "invisible people." A group of researchers from the Netherlands explored the subject of the elderly on the spectrum and found only three papers regarding the topic of late in life autism. Focusing on case studies, the researchers found that the diagnosis of autism including Asperger syndrome is applied after a major life change disrupts their generally predictable daily routines. This sudden upheaval, known so well by us parents, and so vividly described in the current literature, can result in anxiety, depression and irritability, with levels elevated above the normal range.

Another author Joseph Piven, quoted in my earlier chapters, professor of psychiatry at the University of North Carolina suggests that it is not uncommon for adults to come to terms with their own autistic spectrum disorder only when one of their own children receives the diagnosis. Piven's team are looking at the nature of aging with autism as he notes that there is "almost nothing" written about autism among the geriatric population.

Yet another case is illustrated through studies made by David Mandell from the University of Pennsylvania. He states that until the 1980s, persons exhibiting what might be described as autistic behaviors, for example, repetitive body movements, may have been placed in institutions for the mentally ill, with a possible diagnosis of obsessive-compulsive disorder or even schizophrenia. As early as 1943, schizophrenia was an acceptable medical label for a mental illness that was characterized by breaks from reality, such as hallucinations and disorientation. In 2009, under the aegis of the newly created Pennsylvania Bureau of Autism Services, Mandell was tasked with the goal to look for "missing" adults in institutions such as the Norristown State Hospital. At first skeptical, Mandell agreed and set up a diagnostic procedure which was strict and rigorous. His team discovered that nearly 10% of the current residents of Norristown had undiagnosed autism, having received a diagnosis of chronic, undifferentiated schizophrenia. It was no wonder, then, that their treatments were ineffective since they were being given medications for a condition that they didn't have.

A remarkable story was reported about a patient referred to as B. P., who was 64 when Mandell and his team interviewed him. Leo Kanner had actually examined this patient when B.P. was 10 years old and was given the diagnosis of autism, and he had recommended institutionalization since the boy was seen as potentially dangerous. As Mandell and his team studied the stack of records through the years of his institutionalization, they noted that Kanner's diagnosis of autism had literally disappeared. Instead, it had been replaced by the misdiagnosis of schizophrenia for which he received powerful, sedating drugs. When Mandell and his team shared their findings about B.P. and the other nearly 10% of the institutionalized patients, the staff began to wean them off of their medications and treatments, but, as Mandell reported, much irreversible damage had already been done.

A Missing Generation

Leo Kanner is often described as the physician most responsible for coining the term "autistic" to describe a group of children under his supervision. He claims that he was not actually looking for anything in putting forth his diagnosis since, in reality, according to prior statements allegedly made by him, "it was there before." One of the most critical questions raised in the field of autism studies was whether or not the collection of behaviors which defined ASD was unique to the twentieth century, or whether this set of behaviors had gone simply unrecognized, unlabeled and undefined. Kanner often spoke about how in psychiatry the obvious was not recognized until someone observed and described a condition with another set of eyes. He stated that he had actually not discovered autism or as the title of his famous article published in April, 1943, suggests "Autistic Disturbances of Affective Contact" but rather had been at the right place, at the right time, with another set of eyes, with which to observe and describe this phenomenon.

Jessica Wright, writing in a *Spectrum News* article in 2015 (later reprinted in *The Atlantic*), speaks about a missing generation of those on the spectrum, a population which came of age often drugged and living in psychiatric institutions, neglected, ignored and forgotten by their families. She tells the story of Scott, age 55 at the time of the article, who was misdiagnosed with schizoaffective and bipolar disorder and who spent most of his life in institutions and group homes. His mother, Leila Hartman, found out through a psychologist that her son might be autistic and that with such a diagnosis, he may have been able to leave his group home of men who were mentally ill. Scott's diagnosis was finally confirmed in a clinical setting at the University of North Carolina at Chapel Hill. Today, her son lives independently with the support of aids and is, according to his mother, a very different person. Scott was one of the lucky adults who received a diagnosis, albeit very late in the game, still at a point where he could maintain a life of meaning and independence. When Scott was young in the early 1960s, there were virtually no official estimates for the prevalence of autism among children. While many today believe that the rate of diagnosis has substantially increased, evidence would suggest that the actual prevalence may have not significantly risen. This hypothesis is supported by the fact that during the 1950s and 1960s, many children with autism were either ignored or misdiagnosed, as in Scott's case.

On a more upbeat note, Jessica Wright optimistically concludes her article entitled "The Missing Generation" with an anecdote about a nurse anesthesiologist who had received her diagnosis at age 50. Realizing that there were most likely others like her who received their autism diagnosis as adults, she started a support group for adults with autism. It was there that she met her future husband. What began as a deep and fulfilling friendship blossomed into romance, and the two were later married in a ceremony attended by hundreds who had also received their late life diagnosis. At age 50, it was the very first wedding the bride had ever attended.

Jessica Wright is always insightful and current on research topics related to persons with autism. In an article written in February, 2016, she notes what we as parents, as well as researchers, clinicians and health care workers, should now begin to consider in terms of this older population. Describing what autism in the senior adult looks like, Wright contends that once a better, more informed and accurate profile emerges, it can help us apply this knowledge to deal with issues associated with aging.

Managing Health Problems in Adulthood

According to a study conducted by Lisa Croen in 2014 for the Kaiser Permanente in Oakland, California, adults with autism are nearly three times as likely to suffer from depression and nearly four times as likely to have constant anxiety. For reasons which still remain a mystery, these adults are also at high risk for health problems. Mandell contends that these complications, both psychiatric and health-related, can be more debilitating than the symptoms of autism itself. An unexpectedly high incidence of Parkinson's disease has also been described by Piven and a research collaborator from Australia, Sergio Starkstein. In addition to Parkinson's disease, adults with autism appear to have higher rates of diabetes and heart disease, often as a result of poor medical supervision and a lifestyle which overlooks key controls such as weight monitoring and proper nutrition. Compounding this situation, a family physician named Kyle Jones from the University of Utah, notes that many healthcare professionals lack the training and awareness to help adults with autism.

My son was recently diagnosed with what the general practitioner termed as high blood pressure. Somewhat old-fashioned and conservative in his approach, the aggressive physician immediately became concerned about my son's numbers, prescribing statins to lower his cholesterol and medications to manage his blood pressure. The diagnosis of high blood pressure was received by my son with shock and disbelief while his caregivers shared with me, and rightly so, their concern for his immediate care. Using his own logic, he concluded that since he had always lived a healthy life style, the fact that today his blood tests indicate high cholesterol suggest that the numbers are unrealistic and unreliable.

My husband and I were away when the diagnosis was confirmed by another physical examination and additional blood tests. Fortunately, before we left, the tentative diagnosis had already been given to us. Well aware of blood pressure issues, rather than encouraging my son to begin to take prescription medications, I penned a letter to him which essentially outlines a more holistic approach, and included areas for which he needs to assume responsibility such as exercise, lifestyle changes, eating habits, and self-monitoring. He seemed very pleased and mentioned to me that when he gave another doctor he had chosen to replace the original, surlier one a copy of my letter, he smiled. My son mentioned that the letter "saved the day" for him. This was somewhat of an overstatement, but it was a vote of confidence for an alternative strategy to dealing with health issues. He felt that at least someone, his mom, was on his side. Today, I believe that this self-assurance to overcome obstacles may go a long way to instill greater awareness and action in changing his lifestyle. Can he generalize from awareness to action? I am not certain about that, but his family does continue to encourage him and ultimately, to respect his choices.

I fully support traditional approaches to health issues, and do not for one moment pretend to be armed with medical information which can subvert the knowledge of a well-trained specialist. On the other hand, I also believe in choices, alternatives, and taking full responsibility for our own actions when deciding how to best manage medical conditions such as high blood pressure. The literature, scant as it may be for the AS adult patient, suggests a trend in the direction of elevated rates of reported high blood pressure, gastrointestinal issues, diabetes, depression, Parkinson's and anxiety though, as previously noted, too few studies are available to draw conclusions which may lead to better treatment plans.

Noting that medical issues cannot be simply ignored among this aging population, the Chair in Autism Spectrum Disorders Treatment and Care Research dedicated studies to improving the mental health and wellbeing of people on the spectrum in Canada. A research snapshot summarizing some of their findings indicates that — while problems did exist amongst the medical staff treating the older adult on the spectrum — solutions were available, including support and additional training, recognizing that extra time is necessary, importance of family participation and awareness of community resources. In other words, a fairly uncomplicated, commonsense approach would be warranted, and expected by families, for those doctors who willingly accept older persons on the spectrum into their practice.

Incorporating behavioral interventions as part of the diagnostic and treatment plan might help to ease the adult autistic patient into a lifestyle change which can be both satisfying and medically effective. These may include courses in meditation such as Yoga and Tai Chi, supervision by a trained clinical dietician, courses in food purchasing and preparation, as well as therapy to help reduce the social anxiety typically associated with the Asperger syndrome diagnosis. We know that amongst the general aging population, social isolation is a contributory factor in explaining an increase in medical complications. Thus, one can assume that the AS aging adult experiences even more social isolation and withdrawal unless provisions are made to ensure that the person is actively involved in social outings and encounters.

Relationships with those who sincerely care promote feelings of safety and security, a position we have supported and one which was recently affirmed by the people he works with. After receiving the notice about his high blood pressure and high cholesterol, we were touched by how our son was so kindly embraced by both staff and his fellow employees. His new family doctor also made sure to examine him patiently and to encourage his healthy life style, advising him to exercise in order to maintain a good weight level and to continue losing weight. Our consulting psychiatrist reminded us how important the reasonable approach to treating his condition was for him to be able to cooperate and gradually try to let go of his bad habits such as drinking fresh fruit juice several times daily. We slowly, ever so slowly reminded him that this is an exaggerated approach to reaching a reasonable goal and though he continues to argue this point, he is trying to reconcile his interpretation of healthful eating with his medical state. He reads online articles incessantly that are devoted to changing lifestyles, engaging in physical fitness, and being more disciplined about food shopping and cooking. We are pleased by his efforts to inform himself, and that he is accepting some responsibility for his actions. We also hope and pray for a good outcome in the next blood test.

Hard as this is, we recognize how important it is to respect his wishes even though rationally, we understand the dangers of poor health created by overeating and poor dietary choices. We now settle for the fact that he is interested in his health, and at least he is trying to make small changes. We are also grateful that for once, he is neither agitated nor angry; he is not shifting the blame to someone else for his current state of health. This is indeed a very positive step.

Relationships: An Archeological Dig

The recent issue of the Asperger and High Functioning Autism Association, AHA, under the dedicated leadership of Patricia Schissel, April, 2016, describes social skills training workshops entitled Relaxed Encounters sponsored by the Spectrum organization. It appears to be a wonderful opportunity for aging adults on the spectrum who have spent so many years coping with unsuccessful social relationships in both work and personal domains. They note that through consistent repetition, real life encounters and role playing, the ten week sessions can enhance social behaviors by applying strategies to reduce isolation and awkwardness of the AS adult. Missing is any suggestion that such strategies cross age barriers, and what may appear appropriate and reasonable for younger individuals may seem awkward and uncomfortable for older adults. I trust, however, that these age differences do get addressed within the private framework of the workshop, though I do not know that this is a given.

A few years ago, in his self-described frustrated attempts to forge close social relationships, our son compared this process to his work at archeological sites here in Israel. You peel off one layer at a time, he asserted, slowly, methodically and delicately. Still, at the end of this unpeeling process, it remains a mystery if it all fits together! Social engagements and interactions continue to intrigue and challenge him but he seems to be, at age 41, less and less concerned about the outcome than this baffling process. He does not actively seek out social contacts, but he no longer avoids and disdains social encounters either. He often steps aside, observing the interactions from a distance, clearly unsure how to engage but no longer embarrassed to be a quiet observer.

Always a mystery for us. Always the unknown, challenging our rather conventional way of thinking. There are so many questions with ambiguous answers. How much should we intervene in our son's life? How intensely do we try to manage his activities? How much influence do we really have on his choices? Can we comfortably step aside, wishing for the best outcome, no matter what? How significant are the roles we play as his parents and best friends?

And so, my inclination to categorize and chunk life's challenges for my Asperger son seems to demand mental negotiations. When I feel somewhat assured about the decisions regarding the current issue or debate be it related to housing, medical concerns, work opportunities, leisure time or social activities, I feel compelled to rethink and reframe the discussion to be sure I have not missed the obvious, or as Kanner described, to look at something with a different eye. Staying one sprint or step ahead requires total absorption and limitless energy, and as I approach my seventh decade, this is much less realistic. Letting go, then, learning to "go with the flow" in today's jargon, is an approach to living which requires confidence and trust in the institutions and systems set up to monitor and oversee good and fair citizenship.

Finding a Suitable Home

Looking at the status of good housing for people on the spectrum, similar to the situation of health issues and social challenges, the picture is uncertain.

With good intentions, for example, the United Nations declared that reasonable, independent housing choices must be made available to all persons with disabilities. I remain troubled by the lack of decent available housing for the adult on the spectrum. Are we to believe that appropriate and comfortable housing options will always be available for a mature adult with Asperger syndrome? Writing in the May, 2015 health section of *The Atlantic*, Amy Lutz, herself a mother of a severely autistic teenager, writes about a situation in which she says that farmsteads may be a better option for the disabled than the current trend to house in small group, four person size limit homes.

The suggestion that it may be preferable for the autistic population to live in a more diverse, larger farmstead setting, is reminiscent of Donald Tripp's upbringing when he was quite young. The unique Tripp family, who persisted in exploring their options and could afford substantial expenses, found a childless middle-aged couple living on a farm near their own community in Forest, Mississippi, who were willing to house Donald for payment. Though the sum was never publicly revealed, the kindly couple received money not only for his room and board but also for providing him with a safe environment. They even integrated Donald into their daily outdoor routine, giving him training in sowing, cultivating and using a trained horse to assist him with the farm tasks. Kanner himself visited Donald during his stay there, reporting to Mary and Beamon Triplett that the farm represented a kind of therapeutic solution for Donald, given the consistency and structure which gave him a sense of security and a comfortable regular schedule. According to the authors Donvan and Zucker, his time on the farm would always be recounted by Donald as one of the happiest in his life. He was protected and treated with affectionate respect by not one, but two families, sparing Donald the fate of so many autistic people in the US in the 1940s who were condemned to eke out their lives in institutional settings, far removed from their loved ones and familiar environments as was the unfortunate and sad tradition at that time.

Congregate settings, consisting of facilities that house more than the four-person limit, may be ineligible for funding, based on the report issued in 2011 by self-advocacy organizations entitled "Keeping the Promise: Self Advocates Defining the Meaning of Community Living". In the US, the National Council on Disability defined institutional settings as housing in which more than four people live in a single facility. According to recent statistics, the current housing crisis appears to be worsening, at least in the US and most likely in other countries, even excluding Third World or developing countries. More than 80,000 adults on the spectrum await residential placements with a waiting list of up to 10 years. And so, for Americans and by extension, other countries, the question of appropriate housing placement options remains central. Policy debates have continued, as have statewide models and professional perspectives, about the best approach in allocating suitable housing options for the autistic adult.

As reported in the recent *Haaretz* newspaper in Israel, people with disabilities such as autism remain a population at risk for abuse and neglect. Advocating for a network of more than 85 organizations representing adults with autism, Desiree Kameka, the acting national coordinator of the Coalition for Community Choice, describes the situation for direct care as lacking accountability and quality. The staff turnover, nearly 50% as reported by the Israeli press, has a 70% turnover rate according to Kameka.

Additional statistics seem to support Kameka's assertion of neglect and abuse on a national scale. In Georgia in 2013, for instance, 10 percent of those who were moved to community settings died following their relocation. In 2011, an even more frightening picture was described by the *New York Times* which reported that more than 1,200 developmentally disabled individuals had died of "unnatural or unknown causes".

Ari Ne'eman, the founder and president of the Autistic Self-Advocacy Network, became the first autistic person in 2010 to serve on the National Council on Disability. He strongly believes that autistic adults do best when integrated into the wider community, a position we have held in helping to define and maintain a good living solution for our son. Ne'eman told a story about an autistic adult who, along with his caregiver, visited a local pizzeria regularly and when he stopped coming for a period of time, the owner of the pizza restaurant called his caregiver to check up on him.

The term "intentional community" is currently used to describe any planned residential development in which people choose to live together because of certain shared characteristics. Going back to my student days studying linguistics, I am reminded of the term "speech community" which was a term coined by John Gumperz and later revised by both Chomsky and Labov. It was used as a sociological and anthropological concept to describe a group of people who share a set of norms and expectations regarding language use. Medical doctors, for example, belong to a very particular speech community. And so the use of an intentional residential community used to describe a housing paradigm is strikingly similar to the linguistic notion which embraces homogeneity. The question, however, of such a community as being realistic and dependable as a solution for the ASD adult population remains moot. Carefully stating her opinion in the United States Supreme Court decision in 1999 regarding the Olmstead case, Justice Ruth Bader Ginsburg declared that community inclusion may not be right for everyone and that community placement should be determined by state professionals. Thus, one interpretation may be that forcing individuals to live in community settings which clearly do not meet their needs is as much a violation of the Olmstead decision as forcing them into institutional settings.

Segregating and excluding autistic adults remains a topic which is debated among those parents, advocates and community based organizations who truly believe that this is often the best option for those whose disability does not allow them to comfortably reside within the community. And who might then make this determination? Who decides whether or not this choice works best for their children or wards?

Ne'eman's organization and others emphasize the value of ASD adults living in apartments, houses and condos located in communities which have typical public settings including shops, houses of worship, work settings, and accessible public transportation systems. He claims that recent research indicates that people on the spectrum do better when choice and control are provided in smaller settings such as independent living facilities.

Generalizing from this research, it appears that good housing models and outcomes apply more appropriately to persons on the spectrum, like our son, who has an Asperger syndrome, high functioning autism diagnosis, rather than the classic Kanner autism diagnosis. For those on the spectrum who need much more structure and supervision than an independent living arrangement can accommodate, reasonable choices such as homesteads should be considered a good option. Who makes the housing choice and how much supervision and structure is needed remain elusive topics. I do believe that fair and sensible housing options, outside the standard and formidable institutions so commonplace not so many years ago, are reasonable expectations for any civil society in this, the twenty first century.

Entitled to Respect

Since 1952, the American Psychiatric Association's Diagnostic and Statistical Manual of Mental Disorders provided acceptable professional definitions of all known psychiatric conditions. The term "autism" first appeared in the DSM in 1980 and since then, and with each revision, the diagnostic criteria have changed. The term Asperger syndrome was added as a condition along the autistic spectrum or what then became known as high functioning autistic only in 1994. Since then and in the recent edition, it has been merged into the Autism Spectrum Disorder, generating a robust medical and academic discussion about the parameters of the condition.

First we mislabeled our children who were born in the earlier years of the twentieth century. Armed with evidence of their pathologies, they are given psychiatric diagnosis, such as paranoia and schizophrenia, which condemned them to live out their lives abandoned to the miserable custodial care of the state institutions. As more and more parents united to describe the behaviors of their youngsters and look for social and legal support, their movements and organizations evolved into aggressive advocates of change, which included legal recognition of the rights of the disabled. Kanner, Asperger, Bettleheim, Lovaas and Lorna Wing became familiar names associated with the autism spectrum diagnosis.

While there is general agreement that autism has genetic, neurological, biological and chemical components, the degree to which these components interact to create a childhood persistent disorder remains elusive and undefined. Geneticists, neurologists, and others committed to discovering the markers which seem to point in the direction of an autistic diagnosis, are busy at work, fortunately, to help parents to deal with the implications of this lifelong and debilitating condition. Stories of early intervention, which show promise of reducing or even extinguishing the characteristics of an autistic child, offer some hope that certain proven and reasonable approaches are valid and promising. Shedding the dreaded autistic diagnosis, then, can become a much sought-after goal for some parents of these individuals.

But as our autistic children who are not amongst the lucky few who have shed this diagnosis, develop, mature into adulthood and eventually begin to grow old, we as parents experience this sense of despair, fear and aloneness. This is because so little, so very little is known about what the future holds in store for the older autistic population we proudly count as our children. Neurodiversity activists can speak with what some may perceive as a cavalier or smug attitude, coupled with audacity, as they describe a world filled with eccentrics who have much to contribute to society if only their ways could be understood and accepted. Yet others look toward science and medical research to help relieve the pain and suffering they feel is inflicted upon their children. The years that have followed the works of Kanner and Asperger have generated controversial debate about just what defines the autistic. And to some extent, these vigorous and honest discussions are beneficial if they draw a bit of attention away from a world so often caught up in current political upheavals, to focus instead on another dimension of human existence, and develop the empathy to understand and accept those who are unlike the rest of us. As our children age, however, regardless of the severity of the autistic impairment, what we must do now is attend to the needs of this relatively distinct and recently defined population, the aging autistic.

We must initiate a universal conversation about the basic rights of an aging and vulnerable population which, unfortunately, was maligned, ignored and neglected for so many years. This group just happens to include my son. And these human needs I have described, including housing, security, employment, and medical support, demand an enlightened response from the global community which is fair and generous, as befits any moral society in the twenty-first century. We are not characters in a play in search of an author. We are a community of parents who ourselves are getting older, desperately seeking an ideal world that will protect our aging children. A world and a time which, in my humble opinion, might be judged by the manner in which it expresses respect and acceptance of our adult children, who, not because of anything they or their parents have done, just happen to be autistic.

About the Author

Dr. Marlene Ringler is a Ph.D. in English Language and Literature as well as a trained and certified teacher, CEO and founder of the international Ringler English Language Institute. Her company was recognized as a lead vendor for global training for multinationals including Toyota, Intel, IBM, and Microsoft. She pioneered the concept of in-house training specifically in business settings. When living in the United States, Marlene was the co-coordinator of the English for Specific Purposes and English as a Second  Language adult training programs for refugees and immigrants for Montgomery County Public Schools in Maryland. Her program was nominated for special recognition by the White House for its work in adult literacy. An advocate for persons with disabilities, Marlene encouraged people in school systems in the US and in Israel to develop programs for students who might not otherwise be able to function in a typical classroom. She counseled and guided teachers, administrators and parents to recognize the needs of the disabled population. Today, Marlene works closely with service care providers to maximize the potential of the autistic population in a work setting. In addition, she counsels and advises parents about resources, opportunities, and the legal aspects of raising an autistic child to adulthood. Marlene and her family currently reside in Israel and sponsor, host, and organize conferences, social events, and gatherings in order to promote awareness about the needs of autistic adults.

Works Cited

"Adults with Asperger Syndrome at Significantly Higher Risk of Suicidal Thoughts than General Population." *The Lancet Science Daily.* June 24, 2014. https://www.sciencedaily.com/releases/2014/06/140624215940.htm

Alpher, Roger. "Yair Lapid's Tears Don't Help Those With Autism." *Ha'aretz.* June 14, 2016. http://www.haaretz.com/opinion/.premium-1.724781

Asperger Syndrome & High Functioning Autism Association (AHA) April, 2016 newsletter.

Attwood, Tony. *Asperger's Syndrome: A Guide for Parents and Professionals.* London: Jessica Kingsley Publishers, 1998. Print.

"Adolescent Issues for Individuals with AS."*Autism Asperger's Digest.* July/August, 2013. http://autismdigest.com/adolescent-issues-for-individuals-with-as/

"Autism Breakthrough of Knoxville Project," as reported in the *Asperger Syndrome and High Functioning Autism Association Newsletter,* February 2016.

"Autistic People Have Been Abandoned by the State."*Ha'aretz.* Apr 24, 2016. http://www.haaretz.com/opinion/1.715998

Baird, Jennie. "The Other Autistic Muppet." *The New York Times.* Oct. 27, 2015. http://parenting.blogs.nytimes.com/2015/10/27/the-other-autistic-muppet/?_r=0

Ball, Jim. "Housing Options for Adults with ASD." *Autism Asperger's Digest,* July/August 2012. http://autismdigest. com/housing-options-for-adults-with-asd/

Bebinger, Martha. "Troubled Future for Young Adults on Autism Spectrum." *WBUR.* June 09, 2014. http://www.wbur.org/commonhealth/2014/06/09/aging-out-autism-services

"Can the World Afford Autistic Spectrum Disorder?" – interview with Dr. Digby Tantam. http://www.dilemmaconsultancy.org/our-practitioners/sasha-van-deurzen-smith/digby-tantam.html

Also see: dilemmas.org http://www.autismhangout.com/defaultMaint.asp https://www.youtube.com/watch?v=oc7b_5xexkc

Caterall, William. "William Catterall Examines Anxiety Drugs for Autism." *Spectrum*. June 24, 2015. Webinar. https://spectrumnews. org/features/webinars/webinar-william-catterall-examines-anxiety- drugs-for-autism/

Circle of Moms. http://www.circleofmoms.com/

Costandi, Moheb. "Simon Baron-Cohen: Theorizing on the Mind in Autism." *Spectrum*. May 9, 2011. https://spectrumnews.org/news/profiles/simon-baron-cohen-theorizing-on-the-mind-in-autism/

Cutler, Eustacia. *A Thorn in My Pocket: Temple Grandin's Mother Tells the Family Story*. Arlington, Texas: Future Horizons, Inc., 2004. Print.

"Day of Learning 2015"-Alexandra Roth Kahn lecture. Autism Science Foundation. https://www.youtube.com/watch?v=AJ1a-yIcp5Q

Des Roches Rosa, Shannon. "Before Talking about Autism, Listen to Families." *Spectrum*. Jan. 26, 2016. https://spectrumnews.org/opinion/viewpoint/before-talking-about-autism-listen-to-families/

DeWeerdt, Sarah. "For Adults with Autism, Few Good Choices for Treatments." *Simons Foundation Autism Research Initiative (SFARI) Newsletter*, 5-12 May 2015, p. 16. https://simonsfoundation.s3.amazonaws.com/share/sfari-newsletter/2015/20150512nwsltr/20150512sfariNewsletter.pdf

"Over-Synched Brains Trigger Out-of-Step Social Behavior." *Spectrum*, Oct. 22, 2015. https://spectrumnews.org/news/over-synched-brains-trigger-out-of-step-social-behavior/

"In Autism, Brain Responses to Pain don't Match Verbal Ones," *Spectrum*, Oct. 19, 2015. https://spectrumnews.org/news/in-autism-brain-responses-to-pain-dont-match-verbal-ones/

Donvan, John, and Caren Zucker. *In a Different Key: The Story of Autism*. New York: Crown, 2016. Print.

"Autism's First Child" *The Atlantic*, Oct., 2010. http://www.theatlantic.com/magazine/archive/2010/10/autisms-first-child/308227

"The Story of Autism." Wilk News Radio, Laura Lynn Show, Jan., 2016. http://media.wilknewsradio.com/a/112782215/caren-zucker-and-john-donovan-the-story-of-autism.htm

Drori, Jonathan. "Mapping the Needs of People with AS" 2015, Joint Distribution Committee and Ruderman Family Foundation.

Fischbach, Gerald. "Autism Research: Where Are We Now?" Third Annual Day of Learning–April 14, 2016–the Autism Science Foundation. http://autismsciencefoundation.org/day-of-learning-evening-of-celebration/2016-3/

"Fresh Fuel Reignites Asperger's Debate." BioMed Central Limited. *Science Daily*. July 30, 2013. https://www.sciencedaily.com/releases/2013/07/130730235642.htm

Frith, Uta. *Autism and Asperger Syndrome*. Cambridge: Cambridge University Press, 1991. Print.

Gillott, A., and P.j. Standen. "Levels of Anxiety and Sources of Stress in Adults with Autism." *Journal of Intellectual Disabilities* 11.4 (2007): 359-70. Web.

Goode, Erica. "CASES; A Disorder Far Beyond Eccentricity." *New York Times*. Oct. 9, 2001. http://www.nytimes.com/2001/10/09/health/cases-a-disorder-far-beyond-eccentricity.html?_r=0

Gottlieb, Eli. "Adult, Autistic and Ignored." *New York Times* Sunday Review. Sept. 5, 2015. http://www.nytimes.com/2015/09/06/opinion/sunday/adult-autistic-and-ignored.html?_r=0

Gretchen, Carlisle, K., "Pet Dog Ownership in Families of Children with Autism: Children's Social Skills and Attachment to their Dogs." PhD Dissertation presented to the Faculty of the Graduate School of the University of Missouri-Columbia, Dec., 2012. https://mospace.umsystem.edu/xmlui/bitstream/handle/10355/16523/research.pdf

Helles, A., I. C. Gillberg, C. Gillberg, and E. Billstedt. "Asperger Syndrome in Males over Two Decades: Quality of Life in Relation to Diagnostic Stability and Psychiatric Comorbidity." *Autism* (2016): n. pag. Web. https://www.ncbi.nlm.nih.gov/pubmed/27233289

Kendall, Craig. *The Asperger's Syndrome Survival Guide*. California: Vision Research LP, 2009.

Kolevzon, Alex. "Understanding and Treating Anxiety in Autism," Third Annual Day of Learning–April 14, 2016–the Autism Science Foundation. http://autismsciencefoundation.org/day-of-learning-evening-of-celebration/2016-3/

Lee, Yaron. "Tel Aviv Court Rebukes State for Official Use of Term 'Mental Retardation.'" *Haaretz*, February 21, 2016. http://www.haaretz.com/israel-news/.premium-1.704591

"Mentally Unfit for Trial, Israel Has No Place for Them Except Jail." *Haaretz*. May 3, 2016. http://www.haaretz.com/israel-news/.premium-1.717529

Lever, Anne G. and Hilde M. Geurts. "Psychiatric Co-occurring Symptoms and Disorders in Young, Middle-Aged, and Older Adults with Autism Spectrum Disorder." *J Autism Dev Disord Journal of Autism and Developmental Disorders* 46.6 (2016): 1916-930. Web. https://www.ncbi.nlm.nih.gov/pubmed/?term=Lever%20AG%5BAuthor%5D&cauthor=true&cauthor_uid=26861713

Lord, Catherine. "Measures of Success for Adults with Autism Need to Mature." *Spectrum*, Nov. 17, 2015. https://spectrumnews.org/opinion/viewpoint/measures-of-success-for-adults-with-autism-need-to-mature/

Lutz, Amy. "Who Decides Where Autistic Adults Live?" *The Atlantic*. May 26, 2015. http://www.theatlantic.com/health/archive/2015/05/who-decides-where-autistic-adults-live/393455/

Moisse, Katie. "Spotted: Rebranding Oxytocin; Marsupial Madness." *Spectrum*, June 26 2015. https://spectrumnews.org/news/spotted/spotted-rebranding-oxytocin-marsupial-madness/

Moreno, Susan, Marci Wheeler and Kealah Parkinson. *The Partner's Guide to Asperger Syndrome.* London and Philadelphia: Jessica Kingsley Publishers, 2012. Print.

Nuwer, Rachel. "Large Swedish Study Casts Doubt on Autism 'Epidemic.'" *Spectrum*, June 12, 2015. https://spectrumnews.org/news/large-swedish-study-casts-doubt-on-autism-epidemic/

Ozonoff, Sally, Geraldine Dawson, and James C. McPartland. *A Parent's Guide to Asperger Syndrome and High-functioning Autism: How to Meet the Challenges and Help Your Child Thrive.* New York, NY: Guilford Press, 2002. Print.

Packer, Alan. "Startled Fish Help Sound Out Sensory Overload in Autism." *Spectrum*, June 8, 2015. https://spectrumnews.org/opinion/startled-fish-help-sound-out-sensory-overload-in-autism/

Paradiz, Valerie. "Caring for Adults with Autism," NPR, *The Diane Rehm Show.* June 10, 2015. http://thedianerehmshow.org/shows/2015-06-10/caring-for-adults-with-autism

Pelphrey, Kevin. "Kevin Pelphrey Discusses Neuroimaging and Autism." *Spectrum*, Feb. 19, 2014. Webinar. https://spectrumnews.org/features/webinars/webinar-kevin-pelphrey-discusses-neuroimaging-and-autism/

Povey, Carol, Mills, Richard, and Gomez de la Cuesta, Gina. "Autism and Ageing: Issues for the Future" *GERIMED Journal*, April 2011. https://www.gmjournal.co.uk/uploadedFiles/Redbox/Pavilion_Content/Our_Content/Social_Care_and_Health/GM_Archive/GM2_2011/April/AprilP230.pdf

Povey, Carol. "Who Cares? Supporting adults with autism as they get older." The National Autistic Society, 2012. file:///C:/Users/Sandy/Downloads/Who%20cares%20-%20report%20(2).pdf

Powell, Andrew. *Taking Responsibility: Good Practice Guidelines for Services - Adults with Asperger Syndrome*. London: National Autistic Society, 2002. Print.

Raymaker, D. M., K. E. Mcdonald, E. Ashkenazy, M. Gerrity, A. M. Baggs, C. Kripke, S. Hourston, and C. Nicolaidis. "Barriers to Healthcare: Instrument Development and Comparison between Autistic Adults and Adults with and without Other Disabilities." *Autism* (2016): n. pag. Web. http://aut.sagepub.com/content/early/2016/09/22/1362361316661261.abstract

Rudacille, Deborah. "People with Milder Forms of Autism Struggle as Adults." *Spectrum,* Sept. 8, 2011. https://spectrumnews.org/news/people-with-milder-forms-of-autism-struggle-as-adults/

"Invisible people." *Spectrum*. January 27, 2011. https://spectrumnews.org/opinion/invisible-people/

Sarris, Marina. "Daily Living Skills: A Key to Independence for People with Autism." Interactive Autism Network at Kennedy Krieger Institute, April 10, 2014. https://iancommunity.org/ssc/autism-adaptive-skills

Senator, Susan. *Making Peace with Autism: One Family's Story of Struggle, Discovery and Unexpected Gifts*. Boston: Trumpeter Books, 2006. Print.

Shapin, Steven. "Seeing the Spectrum: A New History of Autism." *The New Yorker,* January 25, 2016. www.newyorker.com/magazine/2016/01/25/seeing-the-spectrum

Silberman, Steve. *Neuro Tribes: The Legacy of Autism and the Future of Neurodiversity.* New York: Penguin Books.2015. Print.

Simsion, Graeme C. *The Rosie Project.* England: Penguin Books., 2013.

Solomon, Andrew. "The Myth of the 'Autistic Shooter.'" *New York Times,* October 12, 2015. www.nytimes. com/2015/10/12/opinion/the-myth-of-the-autistic-shooter.html?_r=0

Stephens, Kimberly and Joanne Ruthsatzeb. *New York Times* Sunday Review. "What Prodigies Could Teach Us About Autism," Feb. 27, 2016. http://www.nytimes.com/2016/02/28/opinion/sunday/what-prodigies-could-teach-us-about-autism.html?_r=0

Stevens, Robert J. and Stevens, Catherine E. *Finding Robert: What the Doctors Never Told Us About Autism Spectrum Disorder and the Hard Lessons We Learned,* New York: Square One Publishers, 2015, Print.

Tager-Flusberg, Helen. "Time for Some Soul-Searching in Science." *Spectrum,* Sept. 1, 2015. https://spectrumnews.org/opinion/columnists/time-for-some-soul-searching-in-science/

Tantam, Digby. *Can the World Afford Autistic Spectrum Disorder?: Nonverbal Communication, Asperger Syndrome and the Interbrain.* London and Philadelphia: Jessica Kingsley Publishers, 2009. Print.

"Transitioning into Adulthood," Autism Science Foundation Publication, Feb., 2016. http://autismsciencefoundation.org/resources/transitioning-into-adulthood/

Vermeulen, Peter. "Promoting Happiness in Autistic People." *Network Autism,* May 2016. http://network.autism.org.uk/knowledge/insight-opinion/promoting-happiness-autistic-people

Volkmar, Fred. "Bright Not Broken"-Broadcast in Psychology, *The Coffee Klatch.* 2012 http://www.blogtalkradio.com/thecoffeeklatch/2012/07/26/bright-not-broken--dr-fred-volkmar--yale-child-development

Vought, Janna. *Evolution of Cocoons: A Mother's Journey Through her Daughter's Mental Illness and Asperger's.* Familias LLC, 2013.

Wallace-Wells, David. "A Brain with a Heart" (article about Oliver Sacks), *New York Times* magazine, News and Politics, November 4, 2012. http://nymag. com/news/features/oliver-sacks-2012-11/

Warfield, Marji Erickson, Morgan K. Crossman, Jennifer Delahaye, Emma Der Weerd, and Karen A. Kuhlthau. "Physician Perspectives on Providing Primary Medical Care to Adults with Autism Spectrum Disorders (ASD)." *J Autism Dev Disord Journal of Autism and Developmental Disorders* **45.7 (2015): 2209-217. Web.** https://www.ncbi.nlm. nih.gov/pubmed/25724445

Willey, Liane Holliday. *Pretending to Be Normal: Living with Asperger's Syndrome*. London: Jessica Kingsley Publishers, 1999. Print.

Wright, Jessica. "Adults with Autism Face Old Age without Much Support." *Spectrum*. Feb. 22, 2016. https://spectrumnews.org/opinion/adults-with-autism-face-old-age-without-much-support/

-----""Adults with Autism may have High Burden of Health Problems." *Spectrum*. May 2014. https://spectrumnews. org/news/adults-with-autism-may-have-high-burden-of-health-problems/

-----""The Missing Generation." *Spectrum*. December 9, 2015. https:// spectrumnews. org/features/deep-dive/the-missing-generation/

-----""Questions for Maureen Durkin: Understanding Autism's Rise." *Spectrum,* June 2, 2015 https://spectrumnews. org/opinion/questions-for-maureen-durkin-understanding-autisms-rise/

-----""Genetics: Rare, Common Autism Variants may Function Together." *Spectrum*. April 3, 2012. https://spectrumnews.org/news/genetics-rare-common-autism-variants-may-function-together/

-----""Depression Common among Men with Autism, Study Finds." *Spectrum*. Aug. 24, 2015. https://spectrumnews. org/news/depression-common-among-men-with-autism-study-finds/

-----""Over Next Decade, Cost of Autism could Escalate Sharply." *Spectrum*. Sept. 21, 2015. https://spectrumnews.org/news/over-next-decade-cost-of-autism-could-escalate-sharply/

-----""Questions for Larry Young: Oxytocin's promise for autism." *Spectrum,* April 14, 2015. https://spectrumnews.org/opinion/questions-for-larry-young-oxytocins-promise-for-autism/

-----""Never Mind Statistics: Adults with Autism May be Happy." *Spectrum*, August 4, 2016. https://spectrumnews.org/news/never-mind-statistics-adults-autism-may-happy/

Zeliadt, Nicholette. "Early Autism Diagnoses Stay Stable in 'Baby Sibs.'" *Spectrum*, June 5, 2015. https://spectrumnews.org/opinion/early-autism-diagnoses-stay-stable-in-baby-sibs/

Morgan James
Speakers Group

↗ www.TheMorganJamesSpeakersGroup.com

We connect Morgan James published authors with live and online events and audiences who will benefit from their expertise.

Printed in the USA
CPSIA information can be obtained
at www.ICGtesting.com
JSHW082340140824
68134JS00020B/1793